MASTER MENTORS

SCOTT JEFFREY MILLER

MASTER MENTORS

30 TRANSFORMATIVE INSIGHTS FROM OUR GREATEST MINDS

An Imprint of HarperCollins

Published by HarperCollins Leadership, an imprint of HarperCollins Focus LLC.

ISBN 978-1-4002-2102-8 (eBook)
ISBN 978-1-4002-2101-1 (PBK)

Library of Congress Control Number: 2021937934

Printed in the United States of America
21 22 23 24 25 LSC 10 9 8 7 6 5 4 3 2

TABLE OF CONTENTS

(Continued on following page.)

INTRODUCTION

I'll admit I'm in a bit of an enviable position. Every week I have the opportunity to sit with some of the brightest, most creative, disciplined, and driven people you can imagine and pick their brains for the better part of an hour. They appear as guests on FranklinCovey's weekly *On Leadership* podcast series, which I've had the honor to host since its inception. The series' goal is simple: bring world-renowned experts into an easily digestible, timely, relevant, and inspiring podcast—which has become the largest and fastest-growing weekly leadership podcast in the world.

Conducting the *On Leadership* interviews and reading many of the guests' books has been an experience that often leaves me with a sense of awe and humility. I can honestly say that spending time with each of them and with their respective works has profoundly changed both my professional and personal life. So I wrote this book as an homage to that experience by selecting thirty *On Leadership* guests I've now deemed "Master Mentors," and sharing a single transformational insight from each of them. These insights are often drawn from our interview, but in some cases may have come from a prior or later experience with them. Regardless, the unifying criteria for appearing in this book as a Master Mentor is being a featured guest on the FranklinCovey *On Leadership* podcast series. If you subscribe to *On Leadership*, you'll recognize that our guests share more than a single insight during their interview. However, I wanted this book to be easily digestible and actionable, so I've selected a single insight I've designated as transformational—sometimes against the backdrop of my professional roles as a former corporate officer, team leader, and entrepreneur, and other times through my personal roles as husband, father, brother, son, and friend.

You'll discover that, although the chapters are laid out in a similar format, the content, length, and style of each may read differently. Some are longer and others more succinct. A few even include verbatim transcripts from their interview. Read nothing into those choices. I did my best to represent each person uniquely while creating a cadence that I hope illustrates a transformational insight you'll find valuable and applicable in your life.

I've selected the thirty Master Mentors to cover a wide swath of experiences, challenges, and insights relatable to anyone in a formal leadership role or those working on the self-leadership to move ahead, get unstuck, or open their minds to new ideas and ways of thinking. Depending upon your situation at the moment, some of these transformational insights may hit you as profound, while others serve more as a reminder of what you perhaps already know. Either is fine, as each is beneficial. For a sense of the diversity of experiences and structure you'll find in the pages ahead, consider just a handful of the Master Mentors highlighted:

- Nick Vujicic, author of too many books to recall: His chapter highlights a powerful moment of insight while he was a guest at my home. His example will change you forever.

- Stephanie McMahon, the Chief Brand Officer for WWE: Her chapter speaks very little to the content of our interview, which was superb, but rather to the minutes that led up to her appearance.

- Kim Scott, author of *Radical Candor*, and Trent Shelton, author of *The Greatest You*: These two chapters are fundamentally different from the others in that I included the word-for-word transcript from portions of their interviews so as not to miss any of their voice or nuance.

- Stephen M. R. Covey, author of *The Speed of Trust*: This chapter focuses on an insight and leadership skill I learned from him nearly twenty-five years ago—long, long before the first podcast. Not *my* first podcast, but *the* first podcast.

And those are just five of the thirty Master Mentors included in this first volume. Narrowing from well over a hundred interviews was no minor challenge, and is why there absolutely has to be a second, third, fourth, and ongoing volumes in this series. Looking forward to *Master Mentors: Volume 12* in 2032!

To center the main transformational insight and help it stick in your life, every chapter ends with a summation of the key insight and a question or two to prompt deeper thinking and adoption of the principle/practice. My hope is that in the same way I have made these Master Mentors a part of my life, you'll accept the invitation to do the same. Chances are, there's at least one transformational insight highlighted here that holds the potential to profoundly change your life for the better.

Think of reading this collection of Master Mentors like spreading a bet across all thirty-seven numbers on a roulette wheel. If you're willing to give the ball a spin, you're guaranteed to hit the jackpot.

MASTER MENTORS

NICK VUJICIC

FRANKLINCOVEY
ONLEADERSHIP
WITH SCOTT MILLER

EPISODE 100

NICK VUJICIC

GRATITUDE

Many of the forthcoming chapters in *Master Mentors* feature a particular insight I've taken from either a guest's book or their podcast interview. Then there's Nick Vujicic. There's no such thing as a single transformative insight from Nick. Just being in his physical presence is wholly transformative.

Although Nick appeared virtually on our podcast, as most guests do, several weeks later he was a guest at my home in Salt Lake City, Utah. Although Nick lives in Texas, he was traveling to California and dropped by to join my family and friends for a dinner party of sorts. If you're connected to me on any social media platforms or by chance follow me, you know my family has a tradition of hosting a monthly dinner where we invite someone of unique stature to join us and about fifteen local friends. Each month I invite a mix of local business and community leaders, educators, friends, and professional colleagues to join a featured guest for a few hours of food and conversation. It's been a remarkable experience not only for the invited guests but also for our three sons (ages ten, eight, and six) who meet and sit in on fascinating conversations with celebrities, government leaders, and people we've met who are remarkable in some unique way or have accomplished something truly significant. We've hosted famous musicians, actors, authors, and politicians. A recent guest was former Utah governor and ambassador Jon Huntsman, who ran for the Republican nomination for president in 2012 and served as the United States ambassador to both China and Russia under the Obama and Trump administrations. You could have heard a pin drop during that dinner as he shared stories of his life as a diplomat. Truly remarkable insights are shared each month from different guests.

Nick Vujicic's dinner was even more captivating.

Now, what you need to understand and perhaps be reminded about Nick is that he has no limbs—no arms and no legs. He was born in Melbourne, Australia, with just his head, neck, torso, and a small footlike appendage attached to his waist area that allows him some simple mobility. His "foot" provides him with some pivot capability when he's on the ground and also allows him to text and type. He cannot eat or drink without help. He cannot dress, use the restroom, shower, or even scratch his nose without help. His physical limitations are completely unrelatable to any able-bodied person. I suspect they are also fairly unrelatable even to most people with physical handicaps.

Nick has channeled his physical challenges into a brand of inspiring everyone he meets. He has authored numerous books on his life's journey, his perseverance, his religious faith, and leadership topics that have made him a worldwide celebrity speaking on stages to massive audiences. He told me his largest audience ever was eight hundred thousand people in eastern Europe. Can you even imagine that? I once spoke to seven thousand people and I thought I was the bomb!

Nick Vujicic is the real deal in every aspect. Beyond his physical limitations, most of us can't relate to his influence, celebrity, or constant stream of opportunities from companies, nonprofits, governments, and organizations asking him to speak to their group or represent their brand. In a moment of levity on my living room sofa, Nick confessed, "It's a good life, Scott." The irony was not lost on me, I promise you. But his lack of arms, hands, legs, and feet isn't the feature of his message and legacy. It's his mental attitude of gratitude. And that's the transformative insight I'd like to highlight.

Nick's life is full of gratitude for all he has. He focuses solely on what's ahead, not what's behind; on what's happening now and next, not what's missed or lost. He is a model of what Franklin-Covey's cofounder Dr. Stephen R. Covey would describe as having an abundance mentality. It's actually contagious being in his presence. You can't help but feel some shame thinking about your trivial problems when you're with Nick. But I had the opposite feeling with Nick at my home—an overwhelming sense of gratitude flooded over me. Here's the story:

Nick is sitting on one of the purple velvet sofas in my home, a prominent feature of the many videos I've taped while sitting on them. He's on one sofa and I'm on another sitting across from him. My wife, Stephanie, is sitting next to Nick and we're just chatting before the other guests arrive for our monthly dinner. As Nick is talking about some business opportunities, I find myself lost, looking at his body. Now, I know Nick well enough not to be awkward around him, plus he has a remarkable ability to put everyone at ease as soon as they encounter him. But I am, for perhaps the first time in my life, truly grateful for my hands and fingers—something I notice when I unconsciously retrieve a glass of water on the coffee table and drink from it. Apparently, I am thirsty, but it is all done reflexively. I don't even think about it. It is just so natural—I am thirsty, so I will drink some water. Zero effort on my part.

Do I even need to describe the level of heroic effort it would take for Nick to access some water? If his life depended on it, I'm not sure he could accomplish it alone. At least not in my home.

I may not be adequately describing the insight here other than to say I didn't fully understand gratitude before that day . . . before looking down at the glass of water in my hands. Then, as I put the water down, I took a fuller inventory of all my complacency: my arms and all they do for me, my legs and the mobility they afford me. This sounds dumb, I fear, but I'm now just typing from my heart to relay what has become a newfound sense of gratitude in me.

The doorbell rang, and without even thinking about it, I stood up and walked to the front door to welcome our dinner guests. Walked . . . with my own two legs and feet. Then about ninety minutes later, while we're all outside having dessert and listening to Nick entertain us with some of his most outrageous, blushworthy travel stories, I again thought about my hands. I looked down and noticed I was holding a small dessert plate, putting a fork into my slice of Key lime pie. I looked over at Nick, watching him constantly balancing his torso in his chair while I mindlessly ate my pie. I didn't even remember picking it up to hold it.

I think you get the point by now. Certainly not with every motion, but since my time with Nick in our living room and subsequently at the dinner, I have a viscerally heightened sense of gratitude for what I've completely taken for granted my entire life: my hands and fingers. I can drink a glass of water. Nick can't. I can put a fork into my Key lime pie. Nick can't. I can catch myself if I fall out of my chair. Nick can't. By now I'm sure you're wondering how he even functions. Nick is very resourceful, but he also travels with Giovani, a full-time companion, who nearly invisibly attends to all his needs—a hero in his own right.

To cap this chapter, Nick's life reminds me of something FranklinCovey's other cofounder, Hyrum Smith (creator of the famed Franklin Planner), was known for saying: "I have to. I ought to. I get to." In short, Hyrum proposed there were three mindsets we can choose from in life. I'll use a mundane task we all face daily to illustrate them.

"I *have* to take the garbage out."

"I *ought* to take the garbage out."

"I *get* to take the garbage out."

In the winter evenings here in Salt Lake City, when the wind and snow are blowing at ten degrees and the sidewalk to where our garbage cans are stored is iced over, I'm mindful of Nick. Then I think to myself: *I get to take the garbage out*. I'm sure Nick would absolutely love the chance to do the same. And thanks to his abounding and living example of gratitude, I can say that now I do too.

. . .

THE TRANSFORMATIONAL INSIGHT

Build mindfulness around the small things you take for granted (which actually may be big things) and practice more consistent gratitude in every area of your life.

THE QUESTION

What will it take in your life to transform your level of gratitude from *I have to* or *I ought to* to *I get to*?

STEPHANIE MCMAHON

FRANKLINCOVEY
ONLEADERSHIP
WITH SCOTT MILLER

EPISODE 50

STEPHANIE MCMAHON

YOUR BRAND IS HOW YOU SHOW UP

Recently (prepandemic) I was on the road giving a keynote and living the glamorous life of an author—which typically means speaking at some sort of conference during the day, conducting a breakout session later, then following up with other client meetings when it's over. Having given it your all onstage and throughout the day, you end up fairly exhausted back at the hotel with zero interest in sightseeing. TV and room service become your norm.

This particular evening, *Undercover Boss: Celebrity Edition* had just started. The "boss" was Stephanie McMahon of WWE fame, and that sounded equal parts outrageous and intriguing. The show is a reality series where the CEO, founder, or other senior-level leader goes undercover to meet frontline employees, often under the guise of being a new employee themself. This gives them an intimate look at some of the professional challenges that may go on with the business. It's also common for the employees to disclose issues in their own personal lives that are emotional and even heart-wrenching. Stephanie portrayed herself as a compassionate and empathic executive who sincerely cared about her employees. I use the word "portrayed," as I only knew of her larger-than-life WWE superstar persona. I ended up crying during the episode (I bet you would too), and we booked her the very next day as a guest for *On Leadership*.

Not an avid wrestling fan, I knew little of the popularity of WWE, also known as World Wrestling Entertainment. I'd also heard the McMahon name—Vince McMahon was the founder and public face of the entertainment giant, and his now-former wife, Linda McMahon, was once the president and CEO of WWE, twice a candidate for the US Senate, and administrator of the Small Business Administration. Simply put, the McMahon family knew how to run a business—a billion-dollar business, to be more precise.

Truthfully, I was less familiar with their daughter, Stephanie. I knew she was married to a famous wrestler and that she appeared as an on-screen character in their live events and in a wildly popular television series of the same genre. Besides her public profile as a superstar and in-ring antagonist, I learned she also served as the Chief Brand Officer of WWE and has an impressive commitment to leadership and culture. This caught me a little by surprise, because if you google Stephanie, look her up on YouTube, or watch WWE programming from the last twenty years, it's clear she's built a massive and successful personal brand as the evil corporate titan, putting profits ahead of people and taking advantage of the "everyman" worker to get what she wants. This is the entertainment business, so I didn't take it too literally. But one might think such a convincing act might not be too far from the truth. It's not a stretch—inventory much of Hollywood, and you'll see what I mean.

Was my inclination right? Not even close. Let me explain.

Stephanie captivated me with her brand expertise as I'd just completed my own seven-year tenure as the chief marketing officer for FranklinCovey. Now, you might be tempted to think those two organizations have little in common, but I challenge you to consider your own business: some big personalities, the best-idea-wins brawls in the innovation ring, the flash and bang of marketing, cultural cheers and boos from the stands. Yep, your organization probably has a lot more in common with WWE than you think. It didn't hurt that her experiences as a leader and culture builder at WWE were an outstanding model of what we teach at FranklinCovey either.

Now, I certainly could have used this chapter to share a marketing or brand insight from a Chief Brand Officer like Stephanie. In fact, that was my intention when I invited her to be a guest on the podcast. As I learned more about WWE, I came to appreciate the unparalleled fan loyalty they've built (over a billion social followers) online and at live/pay-per-view offerings (over one hundred thousand people regularly attend WrestleMania events). WWE is now involved in gaming, podcasts, and feature-film production. How they've managed to both keep the "main thing the main thing" and also diversify is worthy of a *Harvard Business Review* case study. Perhaps I'll invite Stephanie to cowrite that with me (like she needs me for that).

Instead of an insight revealed during our on-air interview, I am choosing to feature what she said and how she showed up *before* we taped the interview. Candidly, I kind of wondered about the whole superstar-character thing from the beginning as she was late for our interview. Stephanie's team logged in on time and then graciously told us she was running a bit behind. Now for the record, she's a celebrity and a C-level corporate executive, but we interview big stars weekly and everyone is on time, from Pulitzer Prize–winning authors to four-star generals. We also run on time.

Of course we do—we're FranklinCovey, the global productivity experts. About ten minutes passed and we started to get nervous. All the production crew, myself included, have day jobs at FranklinCovey, and the podcast tapes in the cracks and crevices of our own solidly booked schedules.

Finally, Stephanie appeared. She'd been in a meeting that ran over and was naturally apologetic. Understandable. But what happened next became one of the key motivations I had for writing this book. As someone's grandma has said more times than once, "Sometimes the biggest things are the smallest things." Truth. Once Stephanie was settled and focused on the interview, I was struck by how her attention became all about *us*. For someone adept at playing the role of a superstar, Stephanie's time with me was the complete opposite: zero about her. She was focused on *our* needs, *our* end product, and *our* audience. Stephanie asked where we wanted her to sit in her office. She asked us if the lighting and sound on her end was sufficient. She carefully clarified the profile of our listener and viewer and was palpably invested in delivering for us. All of our guests are courteous, but Stephanie was different—she was confident and clearly invested in and focused on what mattered to *us*.

If I recall correctly, her team had set up a tablet as her device to conduct the interview with. Not ideal, but also not uncommon. After a few attempts to position it properly and some connection issues, she acknowledged it wasn't optimal and, on her own, found a laptop, logged in, and positioned it perfectly for our team. This recalibration alone took another five minutes that, given her day and demands, was no minor investment of time. She made other small accommodations that no listener or viewer would ever know about, but that I carefully took mental note of.

I was so impressed with Stephanie's demeanor before we started taping, I've now committed to integrating it into my own mindset and practices when I join a television, radio, or podcast interview or am hired for a speech. A little recognition or fame can humble the most arrogant of us. And when I say *us*, I mean *me*.

Stephanie's focus—not because she was late, not because she wanted to look good, but because she was serving *us*—is what I'll always remember. Beyond any organizational-brand insights, how she respected the setup changed my own paradigm about one's personal brand. I realized that Stephanie's persona on *Undercover Boss* was the same off-air as it was on. And since the interview, she and her team have been a sheer delight to work with. Although I don't know Stephanie as well as I know many of the other Master Mentors featured here, I remain a fan.

Even more so as I encounter the opposite.

Recently I was interviewing a book author on a different series where I serve as the moderator. Although this author's book has sold well in its particular space, their name recognition, influence, and, frankly, fame was a pale shadow when compared to Stephanie McMahon. This author behaved boorishly to the crew, threw tantrums when certain technologies failed, and generally acted like a diva. It was embarrassing. The author was completely unaware of how their treatment of others was destroying their brand. I couldn't help but think of Stephanie during the entire production—she being an A-lister who acted as un-divalike as possible, compared to an E-lister who expected the world to treat them as if they weren't.

As an expert in corporate and product brands, Stephanie taught me an invaluable lesson about personal brands and the value of showing up as your whole, genuine self and authentically managing your reputation at all times. As she demonstrated that day (and since), when *who you are* graciously aligns with *what you do*, your personal brand will be obvious to all and the envy of many.

. . .

THE TRANSFORMATIONAL INSIGHT

You're always on camera . . . even when you're not. How you look and act is your brand.

THE QUESTION

How much of a scripted "character" are you bringing into your leadership role? Is your motivation self-focused and inward-focused, as opposed to being other-focused and outward-focused?

DAVE HOLLIS

FRANKLINCOVEY
ONLEADERSHIP
WITH SCOTT MILLER

EPISODE 93

DAVE HOLLIS
VULNERABILITY

After thirty years working in the leadership-development and performance-improvement industry, you'd expect that I've learned a few things, including how to squeeze two insights into one chapter. So look for them.

From reading literally thousands of business and leadership books over my life combined with my own experiences leading hundreds of people, I've identified and ranked what I think the top three competencies and contributions required from leaders are. Put aside technical skills and the ability to "run the business" for a moment—both of which are vital—and consider my top three: recruit and retain people who are more talented than you, provide people feedback on their blind spots and areas of growth, and demonstrate vulnerability. And while I suspect Dave Hollis excels at all three, it's his example of demonstrating vulnerability that makes him a Master Mentor in my book.

Brené Brown, a renowned research professor and expert on shame and courage, is likely responsible for popularizing moving vulnerability from a weakness to a strength—or at least making it safe to do so. And I've seen no one demonstrate this strength better than Dave. Among his many contributions, Dave built the organization he and his former wife, Rachel Hollis, created on the success of her brand. Rachel and Dave, with the support of an immensely talented team in Austin, Texas, built momentum with millions of people, including buyers of their books, participants at their live events, subscribers to their blogs and social media posts, attendees at their online coaching courses, and consumers purchasing their related products and tools. In my judgment, nobody has built a faster, more impactful brand than this team. But they did it with a unique approach: they were remarkably vulnerable and allowed everyone to identify with, and learn from, their own struggles. Their genuine openness and accessibility is why I became not just a fan, but a follower and promoter.

Imagine the courage it takes to live your life in public—especially for the purpose of teaching others. And before you label me as naive, I'm well aware of the differences between starring in Bravo's *Real Housewives* series and doing what Rachel and Dave have done. For the record, I see zero comparison. As I've come to know Dave personally, he fueled my own humility and confidence in owning my messes and tapping into the generosity that flows from demonstrating transparent vulnerability. Now, I'm no therapist, but mine tells me I'm on to something here. Having read Dave's first book, *Get Out of Your Own Way*, I feel more empowered to share my wins and losses (there are infinitely more of the latter) in the hope others can learn from my own vulnerability. My favorite insight into Dave's journey came from an email Rachel once sent him midway into his tenure as the leader of their company, The Hollis Co. More on that in a moment.

Before taking the reins of The Hollis Company, Dave had an enormously successful multi-decade career in the entertainment industry. Despite his larger-than-life personality, I'd never heard of him prior to that move. As an executive-level leader at The Walt Disney Company (where I also worked for four years at the beginning of my career), Dave ran a large division responsible for successfully launching their motion pictures around the world. Having worked for Disney, I can imagine his budget, influence, and even the control he had over a large group of associates who executed his vision, strategy, and decisions. Although Disney is a multifaceted organization, movies drive everything: theme park rides, Halloween costumes, television spin-offs, plush toys, action figures, marketing deals with restaurants—it's endless. Movies are vital to every brand extension at Disney, and I bet Dave knew it and loved it. Who wouldn't?!

So, for reasons only he and Rachel truly know, Dave stepped off the Walt Disney Studio compound and into a deconsecrated church building in Austin, Texas. It housed their small but burgeoning team of employees, and I was honored to join them for their first official employee Fireside Chat. I spent the morning in awe as I watched their vision become a reality. I'm not easily impressed, but this was a startup in its truest form—jumping from zero to 200 mph in under two years.

At the time of my visit, I think The Hollis Company had just shy of fifty team members when Rachel sent Dave the aforementioned email—an email from the founder of the company (Rachel), also his wife, to her husband (Dave) who was now the CEO of their joint company, formerly her company. Confused? Let's just say their arrangement was not nearly as simple as my wife's and mine. I earn it and Stephanie manages it. (You thought I was going to write "spends it," didn't you? Shame on you.) We have a simple and clear balance of power in the Miller home. The Hollis home . . . ? Perhaps not so much, given two high-performing and professionally driven spouses working together at the time.

So, Rachel sends Dave an email—a communication technique I think is brilliant for spouses who work together or any business partners who wish to minimize emotional and delivery distraction from their intended message. The email essentially said, "Dave, welcome aboard and wake up. You're trying to lead this company as if you are still on the seventeenth floor of some Burbank office tower. Hello! We've got one floor and fifty people and you need to come down from the safety of your executive cloud and get in the trenches."

I've taken some creative license here, so you can buy Dave's book for the whole story, but the learning for me was profound. Rachel wasn't telling Dave he was lazy, incompetent, or lacked any of the strategic skills needed to grow and navigate this rocket ship known as The Hollis Co. She was instead telling him he should realize the new reality of his new role and he needed to adjust, recalibrate, and reconnect at a different level than he'd become accustomed to at Disney. That meant no executive assistants, no large expense accounts, no multiple layers of leaders. Dave now worked ten feet from the team and they needed him to lead from the same floor. He needed to understand their daily challenges and obstacles, and metaphorically (or some days, literally) roll up his sleeves and move from working "on the business" to working "in the business."

This advice can be counterintuitive for many of us moving up in an organization. There is a distinct need to leave the day-to-day whirlwind behind and become more strategic and intentional as one moves to a higher floor and greater organizational responsibility. Doing so is sound advice. But not always. In Dave's case (and for many entrepreneurs and first-level leaders), there are times we may need to move down the organization, and there's no shame in that. I'll bet Richard Branson (Virgin), Bill Marriott

(Marriott hotels), Arianna Huffington (*HuffPost*/Thrive Global), and others of their stature could share similar stories about their need to stay connected with the soul of their companies. This reminds me of one of my favorite quotes from Randy Illig, FranklinCovey's sales performance leader: "Often we say we have twenty years of experience when in fact we have one year of experience, repeated nineteen times." It's a fact that the best way to continue our relevance is to stay as close to the problems, challenges, opportunities, and realities of our team members as is realistically possible.

So, where does vulnerability show up? It would have been easy for Dave to file the email away and perhaps have an awkward dinner conversation later that night. But Dave used it to teach a transformative lesson by sharing the email from Rachel in his book (which is precisely the reason I know about it).

Vulnerability is a leadership competency. Intentionally sharing your struggles with those you lead or hope to influence is a gift they'll never forget. Whichever rung on the ladder you're on, don't be afraid to step down. Assess how distant you are from where the real work is happening in your organization, division, or team. Has your title accidentally or intentionally separated you from the vital connections and learnings that come from being close to the struggle? As a leader, how much space have you put between you and your team? Are you leading from forty thousand feet or forty feet? (Nobody wants you managing from four feet, by the way.) Dave beautifully illustrates vulnerability in sharing that there even was an email, and further vulnerability in sharing the contents of the email about his tendency to lead from "on high."

This brings to mind the perfect illustration of another vulnerability challenge we all face. Recently, FranklinCovey's president and COO, Paul Walker, shared an insight he learned from one of our internal consultants. It goes something like this: Executive-level leaders and CEOs are paid to think about long-term strategy and the big picture. Many of them spend most of their days ensconced in their private offices, often alone or in their inner circle, refining new strategies. After many iterations, they convince themselves their new strategy is sound and ready to be announced (and often, it is). They then share the strategy companywide in a conference call, town hall meeting, or even fly office to office to communicate the new plan. They then get back on their planes, expecting it all to unfold exactly how they proposed.

Then, from their plane literally and metaphorically thirty thousand feet in the air, they look down and see life in slow motion. They experience what any passenger does at that altitude when looking out the window—the cars, buses, trains, and so on all seem to be moving at a glacial pace. Everything is serene and slow. Too serene and too slow. They wonder and lament out loud to their team, "Why is it taking so long for everyone to execute the plan?" when, in fact, what's really happening on the ground is people are running around banging into each other and obstacles because they are tethered to the plane and being dragged around at 600 mph. It's nearly impossible for them to get their footing with the new direction while still delivering on their current commitments.

It takes the vulnerability shown by Dave Hollis to step off the plane and stick around a bit longer to understand deeply what the reality on the ground is really like. Vulnerability shows up through observable acts of humility. So land that plane, descend from your seventeenth-floor executive suite, and forward that email critical of you so others can learn from it as well. Follow Dave Hollis's example and roll up your sleeves and engage with those you lead. The currency of such vulnerability can improve your leadership prowess, your brand, and strengthen your relationships with others.

. . .

THE TRANSFORMATIONAL INSIGHT

There are two in this chapter. First, recognize that vulnerability is an actual leadership competency, and that peers, colleagues, and direct reports crave relatability and transparency in their leaders. Second, the higher you are in an organization, the more warped and blurred your view becomes of what's really happening on the ground. Remember not only to focus "on" the business, but to work "in" the business as needed.

THE QUESTION

Stephen R. Covey wrote, "Be a light, not a judge. Be a model, not a critic." What actions are required for you to demonstrate the vulnerability that allows those around you to do the same?

SUSAN DAVID

FRANKLINCOVEY
ONLEADERSHIP
WITH SCOTT MILLER

EPISODE 45

SUSAN DAVID
EMOTIONAL AGILITY

FACTS. SO INCONVENIENT. Often they prove me wrong, which is why they're so very annoying. I much prefer my time-honored (and typically disproved) strategy of operating based on my mood, feelings, and opinions. It feels so much more . . . natural.

Relate?

Of course, I don't mind facts so much when they support my position, or on typically black-and-white issues like budgets or processes.

Who am I kidding? I mostly find facts wildly inconvenient, destructive to my ideas, and counter to the narrative I've too often built in my own mind. But I'm a work in progress and willing to learn. Which is why I invited Dr. Susan David on the podcast. A renowned psychologist at the Harvard Medical School, she's also the bestselling author of *Emotional Agility.* Her TED talks have over ten million views, and if you're captivated by a great accent, she's South African (which I rank at the top of the accent food chain). Some of you might vote for accents like Irish, Australian, British, or even New Zealander—but it's my contest and I vote South African as the winner. Listen to her interview with me and tell me it's not distracting—in a good way.

I first encountered Dr. David as a speaker at the World Business Forum in New York City. As I was sitting in the Lincoln Center watching her present, I found her so captivating and her insights so relevant that I ordered her book *Emotional Agility* from my seat. When it arrived, I quickly devoured it. So many insights to be gleaned when you combine a therapist, researcher, speaker, and practitioner. And, as we all know, timing is everything, and I suspect her message spoke to me at the exact right time.

The transformational insight I'd like to share from this Master Mentor relates to a scenario I find myself in far too frequently: the normal conflation of thoughts, feelings, and facts. Each of us has what Dr. David calls an internal chatterbox in our head—our "busy mind," where we build a narrative of a future conversation, often with expected conflict. As a result, we begin to confuse our emotions, opinions, and feelings with facts. Quite simply, emotions and feelings are just that—emotions and feelings. And facts are facts. They're not the same. News flash, I know, but as my friend Colleen Dom so wisely stated, "I'm fully aware of the principle, I've just yet to adopt it into my life." (I will repeat this many more times in this book as it's so relatable.)

According to Dr. David, we have on average sixteen thousand unexpressed thoughts a day and many thousands more that we do express. Add to that the fact our brain often lies to us and is quite willing to lead us off a metaphorical cliff. It can play out as one internal conversation leading to another, so we role-play a coming discussion that hasn't even happened yet . . . and may never. Then when we run into that person on the other side of the imaginary dialogue, we carry all the emotional baggage and behave accordingly.

Have you ever done this? I have a double master's degree in this practice. Sadly, with honors.

So here's how it shows up for me: I'm anticipating a high-stakes conversation on the horizon—might be later in the day or later in the week—and I'm motivated to force it. For the record, some people in my life would say I seek and even enjoy conflict, which is patently false. What I seek and enjoy is clarity and resolution. If I see a storm brewing, whether about a professional or personal topic, I like to address it sooner rather than later. I know from far too much experience that the more I neglect growing storm clouds, the larger, messier, and more difficult the storm will be to resolve later. I like to wrestle hard topics to the ground early and then check them off and move on. Even if I lose the argument or the result isn't in my favor, I want to solve it and focus on something else—I detest wasting my emotional time on lingering conflict. I also believe, likely wrongly, that if I take control of a conversation, the outcome will tip in my favor. Sometimes this works; but like all of us, my batting average may look good in a single game, but when viewed across the entire season (i.e., career or life), not so much.

So, with that preamble, I think about how I plan to address the coming conversation. It's often with my wife, Stephanie, with my leader, or with another colleague at work. I like to get ahead of it and begin building my case; so, with my debating skills in full deployment, I start role-playing the conversation—not only my side but theirs as well. I construct exactly what the other person will say to each of my points, and in a likely hilarious fashion (if one could see inside my head), I master the yet-to-even-happen conversation. This process reveals not only what a skilled orator I think I am but my clairvoyance as I lay out exactly what someone else will say three days from now, point for point, word for word. So, I enter the conversation with my metaphorical gloves on and laced tight. But the other side isn't playing the same sport I've trained for. They're ready for a badminton conversation, or perhaps if things are more intense, Ping-Pong, all while I'm looking for a total knockout—me or them; it doesn't really matter. And if the conversation doesn't flow the way I've so painstakingly prepared for, something must be seriously wrong. Many friends and colleagues who may have experienced this in the past and are reading this now are likely stunned at my self-awareness on this topic, reflecting on the time they brought their shuttlecocks to my UFC cage fight.

Now, before you think I'm a complete sociopath, I don't enter every conversation with this mindset. But I do fully acknowledge that my emotions and feelings nearly always trump the role facts play in my mind. I'm too often building a dramatic narrative based on the outcome I want, and am rarely asking myself the important questions Dr. David poses: "Who do I want to be in this situation? How do I want to show up?" Dr. David helped me realize that far too many conversations turned into arguments because I created a self-fulfilling prophecy—not just for myself, but for the others involved in my choreographed future tirade.

No matter how masterful our role-playing skills may be, we're doing a massive disservice to others by pre-assuming we know exactly what they're going to say. And it bears repeating—often the most skilled role-playing is based on fantasy and not facts. And certainly, for me, it was also based on what I wanted the outcome to be and how that could serve my own agenda.

Fortunately, Dr. David says this is a normal condition for many of us. Breaking free requires that we exercise emotional agility and become mindful of what our emotions and feelings really are. For example, if I'm feeling angry during one of my carefully orchestrated conversations because it's going off the rails, Dr. David suggests reframing the idea of "I am angry" to "I'm having the thought that I am angry." This simple technique allows us to name our thoughts and emotions for what they are and not conflate them with facts, creating a gap for "stepping out" and connecting to the positive outcome we *really* want to achieve.

Since this profound *On Leadership* interview, which I confess to having rewatched multiple times, I've trained a good deal less in the boxing ring. I've tried to assume good intent in the other person and align with Dr. Stephen R. Covey's wisdom that effective leaders, colleagues, parents, friends, and neighbors are more concerned with *what* is right than with *being* right.

So the next time (likely today) when facing a future high-stakes conversation, check your preparation strategy. I'm not advocating you enter the discussion unprepared. That's absurd. But become more intentional with the fact you may be taking role-playing too far. Don't assume you know what's going to happen with the other person. And if you find yourself conflating emotions and facts in the moment, practice emotional agility by mindfully naming them as what they are. You may be surprised at how much conflict in your life is self-created and can be lessened if you simply prepare a bit less. Not exactly the wisdom you'll find in most leadership books, but I do think it's a truly transformational insight.

. . .

THE TRANSFORMATIONAL INSIGHT

It's human nature to confuse our emotions, opinions, and feelings with facts. The more aware you are of this challenge, the less you will do it. Both are legitimate, but they serve different purposes, so don't conflate the two.

THE QUESTION

How do you find your own healthy balance between preparation (role-play) and impromptu (winging it) to ensure your next interpersonal engagement is less contentious and more rewarding and productive for both parties?

DANIEL PINK

FRANKLINCOVEY
ONLEADERSHIP
WITH SCOTT MILLER

EPISODE 10

DANIEL PINK
PEAK, TROUGH, AND RECOVERY

I FIRST MET Daniel Pink a decade ago in California. I stalked him for months and convinced him to sit for an interview with our Chief People Officer, Todd Davis. He was exceedingly gracious and fun to work with. I recall I'd carefully managed every detail of the interview, except where we'd tape it. Just a minor nuance that resulted in Todd, Daniel, a film crew, the hotel manager, and I roaming the massive property for thirty minutes looking for a room, hall, quiet nook, or any open space to tape the interview. I'm sure I looked like an idiot—an idiot stalker, to be more precise.

Daniel has hopefully forgotten about the "treasure hunt" interview (all ended up going well in the end), and we've stayed connected over the years. Daniel authored several bestselling books during that time, including *Drive*, *To Sell Is Human*, and most recently *When*. In all of my experience with bestselling authors, Daniel is the model to follow. He channels his passion for a topic into several years of discovery, interviews, and research culminating in such focused and insightful writing, it results in bestseller after bestseller. Seems simple enough, but you try dedicating thirty-six months to a single, all-consuming project and see your results. I'd go sideways around month seven. Perhaps that's the difference between Daniel Pink and Scott Miller. One difference.

Shortly after the release of *When: The Scientific Secrets of Perfect Timing*, I interviewed Daniel to glean his latest thoughts on the value of timing. He shared a litany of fascinating insights regarding the best time of day to appear before a parole board (I'd offer the best time is *never*), what time you should schedule your elective surgeries, the most likely time for car accidents, and, generally, when people deploy their best and worst thinking and judgment. Daniel spoke of the circadian rhythm, which is the twenty-four-hour period of our lives within which we typically sleep for about eight hours at night and are awake for the remaining sixteen during the day. This cycle is led by the hypothalamus. But about 20 percent of people have a chronotype (an individual's proclivity for earlier or later sleep timing) that doesn't follow the formula.[1] That means about one in five have a different operating rhythm and many end up as proverbial night owls, often identified by their distinctive hooting (texting) at 2:00 a.m.

I would most certainly *not* be in that 20 percent. I'm like a baby in that I wake early, immediately exert insane amounts of energy, peak fast, and then recover later in the day. Okay, I'm like a baby in more ways than that, but this chapter isn't about my maturity level, brief attention span, or emotional outbursts (I've already admitted that in the chapter featuring Harvard psychologist Dr. Susan David).

In *When*, Daniel shares a simple yet profound concept called *peak, trough, and recovery*. Where have I been that it took fifty-plus years for me to understand how this concept impacts the effectiveness of my leadership, not to mention the engagement and results of the team I lead? Daniel explains that our peak is when we're highest in our vigilance, typically early in the day when our ability to "bat away distractions" is easiest. This is the best time to perform analytic work (the items that require a laser focus and our full attention). During the trough, which is typically early- to midafternoon for most, it's the worst time for performance and attention, and we should be focused on administrative work (answering routine emails—or, in my case, attending the CEO's boring update meetings, which are always just after lunch). Then comes the recovery later in the day when our energy and moods rise again and we can determine what to focus on. Daniel even mentioned that he purposely agreed to a 4:00 p.m. *On Leadership* interview because he knew a conversation at 2:00 p.m. would not leverage his best energy and thinking.

And that was the precise moment I learned of this transformational insight.

The concept of a peak, trough, and recovery was not a news flash, but the idea of deliberately organizing my day by scheduling certain types of meetings and conversations around my own circadian rhythm definitely was. Until Dan's interview, I'd just accepted appointments and made commitments when there was an open time on my schedule. Plan the next year's fiscal budget with the CFO at 1:00 p.m. because that's when you're both open, even though it's dead in the middle of my trough . . . ? No problem. Ask me to attend a webcast for professional development in the early morning when I should be bringing my best creative energy to designing a global product launch . . . ? Count me in. Join a two-hour meeting with a technology-intensive vendor at the end of the day . . . ? Genius!

Daniel gave me permission—a mandate really—to rethink my entire day based on my own peak, trough, and recovery. Now, I get that my tenure and level in the firm afford me more latitude in owning my daily schedule, but this awareness changed how I organized my day in better alignment with my own rhythm and energy. Here's a glimpse into my life, in the hope it will motivate you to look at and more intentionally own the sequence of your day:

4:00 a.m. wake up	I automatically (or at least with little effort) rise early, especially in recent years when I've been authoring two books annually, producing a weekly Inc.com column, reading a full business book for the weekly podcast interview, and, oh yeah, fulfill a fifty-plus-hour-a-week role as an entrepreneur and advisor for FranklinCovey. As a global company, our businesses in Asia, the Middle East, and Africa are winding down, and it's the time they can catch up with a leader from HQ in Salt Lake City, Utah. (Tokyo, for example, is fifteen hours ahead of me, so the window each day is very short if we need to connect.)
5:00–5:30 a.m.	Writing or working with international partners. It's also common for the CEO, Bob Whitman, to text me and ask me to call him. Bob, like me, is a ridiculously early riser (I think it's closer to 3:00 a.m. for him), and he and I have an implicit agreement that there are few boundaries in the morning. But this is offset by strict (though not immovable) boundaries in the evening.
5:30 A.M. PEAK	
5:30–7:00 a.m.	Writing (until our three sons bound out of bed and get some snuggling and talk time). My hallmark of contribution is my creativity and mental processing speed, both of which are palpably better early in the morning.
7:30–11:00 a.m.	Full on for FranklinCovey and my role as an entrepreneur outside the firm. If you look at those colleagues on the team I lead, it's those who rise early and engage with me first on my schedule who get my best contribution.

11:00 a.m.–1:00 p.m.	Still pedal to the metal, I start thinking about lunch. And when I say thinking, I mean obsessing. I'm one of those old-fashioned (I mean old) kind of guys who needs three squares a day. I can push my mental focus and creativity until about 1:00 MST when there's only an hour left until the NYSE bell rings and I am out. Not Italian or Spanish "out" as in close up the shop, go home, and nap riposo or siesta style; just don't call on me in a meeting for my best contribution.
1:00 P.M. TROUGH	
1:00–3:00 p.m.	Administrative tasks and other necessary items on my "to-do" list.
3:00 P.M. RECOVERY	
3:00–5:30 p.m.	Sufficiently engaged; I come back around midafternoon and fake it well enough until it's time to wind down. Anyone who's ever worked with me knows to line up early.
5:30–8:00 p.m.	Family and parenting time.
8:00–9:30 p.m.	Finish writing and other unresolved tasks. I'm always lying semiflat by 8:30 p.m. with my laptop, books, or a tablet on my lap. The CEO wouldn't call me during this time, as he knows I'm sliding out of parenthood and into bed. I would answer, of course, if he did; but he never does.
9:30 p.m.–4:00 a.m.	Deep coma (except for two to three quick and forced interruptions that come with being a fifty-three-year-old man) until morning, and the cycle repeats.

One thing about my schedule: I want breakfast for breakfast, lunch for lunch, and dinner for dinner. I do not miss meals for any reason during the day, and all my colleagues know it. I am, however, perfectly willing to meet during breakfast or lunch, though rarely dinner.

I also recognize that in parsing out my own time and activities, there are still those 20 percent who follow a different rhythm. One member of my team has well earned her own start and finish times after thirty years with the firm. She begins late (compared to most) and goes late into the evening. Great for her; she deserves it and overdelivers on her commitments. But we pass like ships in the night. And when I say night, I mean day. Her rhythm and peak are the opposite of mine. She gets in the saddle around 9:30 to 10:00 a.m., just as I'm starting to think about my Chicken Fettuccine Alfredo (salad, not soup, please; and bring on the endless breadsticks, as I need the carbs to ensure my midafternoon trough happens). Hmm . . . maybe I just discovered something, but I digress.

This exceptionally competent colleague seems at her best between 1:00 p.m. and 7:00 p.m. When the rush of emails from her stellar results start slamming into my inbox around 5:00 p.m., they go largely ignored. Had they come in around 8:30 a.m., I would treat them like the daily presidential briefing (well, perhaps how it was treated historically). This individual gets the least of my leadership contribution for certain. However, since learning from Dan, we've both tried to become more intentional about our crossover hours, and it's certainly worked better. But generally, we are who we are, and the more we acknowledge it, lean into it, and talk about it transparently, the more we can make accommodations so each of us gets, and gives, more of what we need from each other.

As leader and team member, Dan's role as a Master Mentor has helped me tremendously. I have gone so far as to share with the team when my energy and creativity are at their best, then work to spread that among all the members. And, equally as important, I've been able to influence them to be mindful of their own peaks and troughs, and encourage everyone to work in the ways that best leverage their natural, and largely inescapable, rhythms.

. . .

THE TRANSFORMATIONAL INSIGHT

The more self-aware you are about your circadian rhythm, the better aligned you can be with everyone in your life—professionally and personally.

THE QUESTION

Have you identified the rhythm that leads your day? And can you create increased congruence with those high-leveraged demands that require your best thinking during your peaks and not your troughs?

KAREN DILLON

FRANKLINCOVEY
ONLEADERSHIP
WITH SCOTT MILLER

EPISODE 23

KAREN DILLON
DELIBERATE VS. EMERGENT STRATEGIES

YOU MIGHT AGREE that becoming the editor of *Harvard Business Review* is the pinnacle of a career in business thought leadership. Add authoring the seminal book *HBR Guide to Office Politics,* and you firmly stake your position in the leadership and authoring space. Add to that coauthorship on numerous bestselling books with the late, incomparable innovation expert Clayton Christensen, and nobody sane is questioning your chops. In fact, people gather around the world captivated to learn from your research, insights, and own career experience.

Am I talking about myself? Don't I wish. I'm referring to Karen Dillon.

In fact, she's the opposite of me. Humble. Quiet. Deliberate. Thoughtful. Wise. I could keep going, but I'm quickly feeling bad about myself.

I met Karen several years ago when FranklinCovey's CEO and Chairman, Bob Whitman, was engaging in some writing efforts for the firm. Even the most talented of professionals sometimes have side hustles, and Karen occasionally takes pity on us and offers guidance on our company's writing. It's truly remarkable to listen to her insights after she has reviewed a manuscript or an article of ours and suggests subtle changes that can transform a chapter—or an entire manuscript—and bring it to life in a way we never envisioned. To quote my friend and speaking coach, Judy Henrichs, "Experts *make* it look easy. Novices *think* it's easy."

Karen has authored or coauthored four significant books including *Competing Against Luck*, *The Prosperity Paradox*, and the must-read masterpiece *How Will You Measure Your Life?* which takes proven business principles and teaches the reader how to adopt them successfully into their personal life. The book, coauthored with Clayton Christensen and James Allworth, is a top book recommendation of mine. So, naturally, we invited Karen onto the podcast to share her genius. Although Clayton was a member of FranklinCovey's board of directors for more than a decade, his declining health prevented him from joining her. Sadly, he passed in 2020 after many health challenges, but left a legacy and contribution to our world that is rivaled by few.

The genesis of *How Will You Measure Your Life?* came from a class Clayton taught at Harvard Business School. That led to an article Karen helped edit for *Harvard Business Review*—one of the first articles ever placed on their site to go viral. It is still one of the most viewed articles in the publication's storied history. Clayton didn't just want his students to have an exceptional career, but to have an exceptional life. He helped ensure they navigated many of the challenges all of us face in our careers, legal and otherwise—and especially so in C-suite and executive-level roles.

Karen will tell you that in her nearly ten-year collaboration with Clayton, it was the profound insights in this article and the subsequent bestselling book that led her to make significant changes in every area of her own life. I can't think of a better book to pick up and read when you finish *Master Mentors.* Note: I said when you *finish*, people. Stay focused!

Of the treasure trove of information in their book and Karen's podcast interview, one transformational insight clearly stands out to me. And it's actually drawn from a third-party research study quoted in the book. The big idea: understanding the difference between a deliberate and an emergent strategy.

Karen shares that most successful companies ultimately employed a different strategy than the one they initially launched with. Simply put, success is never preordained. If you succeed, you will most likely let go of your original strategy. In fact, HBS visiting professor Amar Bhidé conducted research on this exact topic and said, "93 percent of all companies that ultimately become successful had to abandon their original strategy because it was not viable."[1] That's remarkable; only 7 percent of companies that achieve success do so with their initial, deliberately laid-out strategy. The vast majority need to pivot, abandon, and adopt a new strategy somewhere midcourse.

But that isn't the only insight on the topic. What I think is especially profound is that, with this knowledge, leaders must carefully calibrate all of their resources. If you know statistically that you're likely to move off your genius idea and, at some point, adopt a wiser, sounder, more resonant strategy, you need to hold in reserve a certain amount of resources to ensure the emergent strategy does in fact succeed. It's a delicate balance of time, effort, focus, and financial resources. On one hand, with this knowledge, you could become so cautious and convinced nothing you launch out of the gate will succeed, you'll hold back on your precious resources for the yet-to-be-identified emergent strategy and starve the initial deliberate strategy to death. Or, conversely, you're aware of this conundrum, but you still go all in (like nearly all of us) on your initial idea. Why go all in? Because it was your idea, and we all have massive egos attached to the success of our own ideas. The first iteration flops and you learn an immense lesson from that humbling, but everyone is exhausted, distracted—or worse, likely out of runway and cash.

As transformative as Karen's ability to share the lessons on recognizing the balance between a deliberate and an emergent strategy is, I think it's equally insightful to plan for it. Not plan for failure, but plan for emergent opportunities to present themselves, hopefully quickly, and plan to be nimble enough to see them coming. That way, you can execute on them with intentionally reserved resources.

In retrospect, I've seen this many times in my career. I'm fond of the adage "Go big or go home." I'm even more fond of "Go big or don't even come." When I go big, it's *big*. As the chief marketing officer for FranklinCovey for nearly seven years, I was well known, to quote a sports phrase, for "leaving it all on the field." And our team's record was quite remarkable—something I write about in *Marketing Mess to Brand Success: 30 Challenges to Transform Your Organization's Brand (And Your Own).* But there were most definitely times when I was humbled and forced back to the drawing board to rethink the plan . . . at the last hour or when the team was exhausted and had nothing else to give. I'm not exactly sure what I would have changed in hindsight, but this knowledge will most certainly impact how I plan for future entrepreneurial ventures of my own. Give it your all while saving some for the inevitable pivot.

Recognizing the crucial need to detach my self-esteem and ego from my ideas, Karen taught me that humility flows from confidence. Confident leaders can demonstrate humility. It's arrogant leaders who can't summon the humility to see their genius must-succeed-at-all-costs strategy isn't working. It's in this humility where leaders, often with enormously successful track records, need to demonstrate the capability to *see* the emergent strategy—

which may come from unexpected sources, including their competition, nemesis, or even the mailroom clerk or receptionist.

. . .

THE TRANSFORMATIONAL INSIGHT

Effective leaders intentionally build a culture where multiple strategies can thrive interdependently and exercise the humility and confidence to see the signs when it may be time to adapt.

THE QUESTION

What will prevent you from moving off your deliberate strategy onto an emergent strategy? How will you know it when it's time?

ANNE CHOW

FRANKLINCOVEY
ONLEADERSHIP
WITH SCOTT MILLER

EPISODE 30

ANNE CHOW
WHAT'S YOUR MOTIVE?

One of my earliest career memories comes from my tenure at the Disney Development Company. I've termed it the "comparison conundrum." After attending a company town hall meeting, I mentioned to my mother how well spoken my peers were when they asked questions of the president. I admitted that, for my part, I could barely understand what he was saying, let alone ask him an articulate question in front of everyone. I recall her advice as if it were yesterday: "Scott, don't compare yourself to anyone else. It's a trap you'll never get out of. Focus on you." I was twenty-four at the time and considered parental wisdom as pretty much stupidity. Oh, how I wish I'd been smarter back then so I could have adopted this and other advice much earlier.

I'm not sure how well I've done at this, but I've certainly stopped trying to compare myself to the incomparable Anne Chow. Name doesn't ring a bell? It will. Talk about a Master

Mentor on the rise, Anne serves as the CEO of AT&T Business, leading thirty-thousand-plus associates and a $36 billion division of AT&T. On its own, the division would be a Fortune 100 company. Anne and I are roughly the same age, and like me, she's dedicated nearly her entire career to one company—thirty years at AT&T. An engineering major at Cornell, Anne also attended Juilliard Pre-College, serves as a member of FranklinCovey's board of directors, and is coauthor of the Amazon bestseller *The Leader's Guide to Unconscious Bias: How to Reframe Bias, Cultivate Connection, and Create High-Performing Teams. Fortune* also named her to their 2020 Top 50 Most Powerful Women in Business, where she debuted at #44.

When inventorying my most recent accomplishments against Anne's, mine include mowing the lawn, writing a blog post, and successfully (I think) taking a shower each day. At this pace, I'm crushing it . . . if I were still in high school (which my wife thinks I may be).

Kidding aside, Anne is a powerhouse and exhibits extraordinary wisdom, even though she is often a decade younger than many leaders at her level. My sense is we will see Anne continue to play an influential role in global business and become a recognized name for her own thought leadership. Anne is also Asian American. Her parents immigrated to the United States from Taiwan fifty-plus years ago, and no doubt their journey has shaped her own.

As a former officer and member of the executive team at FranklinCovey, I came to know Anne mostly in a professional capacity. Over time, as I worked more with her, we developed a friendship—recognizing the uncrossable line between board member (her) and employee (me). As I led our company's thought-leadership initiatives, including our book strategy with my colleague Annie Oswald, I saw how Anne could become a valuable spokesperson for our company on issues that tapped into her passions and leadership experience.

Enter *The Leader's Guide to Unconscious Bias*—the book recently released by FranklinCovey that brilliantly and comfortably sets forth how to identify in ourselves our own biases and then become more self-aware about what to do about them. The premise of the book is that to be human is to have bias, and that not all biases are bad. But developing a refined awareness of when it's negatively affecting others, and yourself, is key to becoming a more effective and trusted leader. As an editor on the book, I read it three times before release, and it's superb. This is a topic with no shortage of opinions. As a white man in my fifties, I entered it a bit guarded, thinking I was going to be shamed and schooled. The opposite happened. I learned a tremendous amount about my own journey, personally and professionally, and how to understand that my experiences, mindsets, and ensuing biases might be limiting to those around me, or when acknowledged, checked and challenged to support and grow others. I highly recommend you buy and read the book.

There's one story in particular from the book that not only had a profound impact on me but changed the way I speak on a certain topic—so much so, I've designated it the transformational insight for this chapter. It's something we all have experience with, on one side or another. Namely, the *motive* behind asking someone where they're from.

Although 100 percent American just like me, Anne looks different from me. Look at me, and I'm a fairly typical white American male in his fifties (although I've long since retired all my khakis after living in Europe and realizing only Americans wear khakis). Anne is Asian. A less traveled person might wonder if she's Korean, Chinese, Japanese, or some other race from the Asia-Pacific region. As I mentioned earlier, Anne's parents were born in Taiwan. That would make Anne's ethnicity Taiwanese, in case you're not clear on that point.

So here's how Anne recounts how the "Where-are-you-from" conversation typically goes. For demonstration purposes, I'll use the name Scott:

Scott: "Anne, where are you from?"

Anne: "I live in the Dallas area."

Scott: "No, where are you really from?"

Anne: "Oh, you mean, where I grew up? I'm from New Jersey. I'm a total Jersey girl."

Scott: "No, where are you *really* from?"

Anne: "Oh, you mean where was I born! I was born in the Midwest."

Now, after hundreds of these conversations, Anne knows exactly what the other person is searching for. They want to know her ethnicity. They perhaps subconsciously, or even consciously, are determining how to relate to her. And this is the part of the unspoken interpretation of the conversation that rocked me, because what Anne was hearing was often, "You're not from here. You don't belong here, and I'm trying to make some sense of it and how I deal with you."

Now those aren't Anne's exact words, but the insight is profound. Admittedly, I've been on the Scott side of that conversation countless times and on the Anne side of the conversation exactly zero times. Certainly people have asked me where I'm from, but it's contextually rooted in where "like me" are you from in *America*, not where "not like me" are you from in the world.

Anne acknowledges that, earlier in life, she might have been less patient or diplomatic during such discussions, and now that she better understands the biases involved, she can use the dialogues as a teaching opportunity. Leadership in action.

I don't know exactly what you're thinking right now, but I hope it involves some introspection. Which was my reaction when

Anne first shared this engagement with me on the podcast. She expands on it further in the book, and since reading it, I've become more mindful of my motives—mainly before I flip into question-asking mode, which is my default communication strategy when I'm socially uncomfortable or rattled with silence. When I feel the need to "move the conversation along," which my wife tells me is always, I ask questions. I've thought of it as generous and well intentioned, but I've become more mindful of my motives since learning from Anne. Why am I asking questions? Why am I asking these specific questions? How do I plan to use the information? That last one haunts me. How do I plan to "use" the information? I have on countless occasions asked people who don't look like me, "So, where are you from?" I don't think I've ever asked someone who looks and talks like me where they are from. I don't need to. To me, they're from "here"—just like me, so all is well. They belong here. Like I do.

When you ask where someone is from, which can be a common default question, you may be drawing on some deeper, unconscious bias. This can be heard as "I'm educated and you're not," or "I'm successful and you're less so," or as Anne experienced, "I'm from here and you're not." Such a distinction can alienate and harm not just the other person, but the foundational trust in the relationship. The sign you are doing this right—which is the same advice my speech coach gave me on mastering movement and speech onstage—is that nobody notices. You don't get credit for doing it right. But you will certainly get penalized—and worse, risk damaging a relationship—if you get it wrong.

• • •

THE TRANSFORMATIONAL INSIGHT

Our motives are commonly driven by our mindsets and belief systems, and are manifested in our language and behavior. Become more mindful of how these are showing up in your life.

THE QUESTION

If you're tempted to ask, "Where are you from?" what could you ask instead? But be sure to address your motives by addressing how you intend to use the information.

CHRIS MCCHESNEY

FRANKLINCOVEY
ONLEADERSHIP
WITH SCOTT MILLER

EPISODE 14

CHRIS MCCHESNEY

KEEP A COMPELLING SCOREBOARD

If Tony Robbins and Richard Simmons had a love child (apologies to their respective spouses/partners), Chris McChesney would be the result.

More explanation needed? Let's just say Chris has a level of indefatigable energy the likes of which you've never experienced and would force the Energizer Bunny into early retirement. Which has been an invaluable asset in his thirty-year path to becoming the world's leading authority on strategy execution.

Chris's three-decade career at FranklinCovey, other than a year's sabbatical working for a popcorn company (different chapter, different book), has been obsessively focused on understanding and solving one business issue: How do organizations execute business strategies that require a change in human behavior? Chris's journey, like many influential teachers, leaders, and respected experts, centers on solving a singular, seemingly intractable problem. For Martin Lindstrom, that focus is on understanding buyer behavior; Seth Godin is arguably the world's expert on marketing; for Brené Brown, it's the topic of vulnerability and being your authentic self; for my sage colleague and Dr. Covey's longtime friend, John Maxwell, it's an unrivaled focus on leadership. When it comes to strategy execution, Chris McChesney takes front and center.

Chris's decades of up-close work with thousands of clients in every business sector has resulted in a trove of insights that culminated a decade ago in his first book, *The 4 Disciplines of Execution.* Coauthored with Jim Huling and Sean Covey (author of *The 7 Habits of Highly Effective Teens*), Chris's book is the bestselling work for building a culture of execution inside your organization. It isn't a book about helping you craft your strategy—call McKinsey or Accenture for that. But if you want help *executing* your strategy, call FranklinCovey and Chris in particular.

After ten years in publication and close to one million copies sold, Chris and his coauthors updated their book with new insights and lessons learned. Same 4 Disciplines, but an entirely new level of understanding about the drivers of executing strategy. For those who may have missed reading the book, here's a short primer on the 4 Disciplines (I'll dive deep into Discipline 3 as the transformational insight for this chapter).

Chris proposes (who am I kidding . . . Chris doesn't propose anything to anyone; he shouts from a mountaintop) that in attaining your Wildly Important Goals, the role of the leader in the business-execution process is critical. His research shows execution breaks down in four ways:

- Leaders and work teams rarely know the goals, so **Discipline 1** is: **Focus on the Wildly Important**. Exceptional execution starts with narrowing the focus—clearly identifying what you must accomplish or nothing else really matters that much.

- Leaders and teams don't know what to do to achieve the goals, so **Discipline 2** is: **Act on the Lead Measures.** Twenty percent of activities produce 80 percent of results, so the highest predictors of goal achievement are the 80/20 activities identified and codified into individual actions and then tracked fanatically.

- Leaders and teams don't keep score, so **Discipline 3** is: **Keep a Compelling Scoreboard**. People play differently when they are keeping score, and the right kinds of scoreboards motivate individuals to win.

- Team members don't hold them themselves and others accountable, so **Discipline 4** is: **Create a Cadence of Accountability**. Great performers thrive in a culture of accountability that is frequent, positive, and self-directed. Each team should engage in a simple, weekly process that highlights successes, analyzes failures, and course-corrects as necessary.

I think Discipline 3: Keep a Compelling Scoreboard is absolutely vital for organization-wide engagement. In recent years, engagement seems to be the word we're all focused on. Every doomsday workplace study shows a "crisis" in employee engagement. Candidly, I pay little attention to them anymore, because if you believe what you read, you'd fold your cards and go home. For example, a recent study from Gallup showed 53 percent of employees "weren't engaged" in the workplace.[1] Another study reported 84 percent of employees would consider leaving their current jobs if offered another role with a company that had an excellent reputation.[2] Seriously? Only 16 percent of the workplace would stay in their current role because of their level of engagement? Good grief. Opportunistic pigs!

In my own professional experience, visual engagement (i.e., scoreboarding) is a key contributor to overall engagement. It's vital to knowing if we're winning. It answers the timeless question: "Are we there yet?"

I'm quite passionate about scoreboarding, but *never* in Excel. Scoreboards should be fun, engaging, and even a bit outrageous. If people aren't talking about your scoreboard, then it's not working. What do I mean? Join me on a journey when, for several years inside FranklinCovey, I led our scoreboarding efforts. Now, the authors of *The 4 Disciplines* book might have been insulted or even horrified at the latitude I exercised, but the team I led in marketing took scoreboarding to new levels (I didn't say high levels, people . . .).

One of FranklinCovey's well-known hallmarks is that we're . . . shall I call it . . . conservative. Not 1980s IBM/Don't-leave-your-desk-without-your-suit-coat-buttoned-and-what-were-you-even-thinking-wearing-a-blue-shirt conservative. Even though now FranklinCovey is a global, public company with rich diversity, its roots are from Utah—not exactly the most progressive state in the union. In many ways the company's culture does reflect that of the state as we have a bit of a conservative bent, which is exactly why my scoreboards were viewed as a bit outrageous inside the firm. Not Snooki-and-the Situation-*Jersey Shore*-how-can-I-make-a-bigger-ass-of-myself-on-TV outrageous, but certainly closer to that than IBM on the other side of the conservative continuum.

At FranklinCovey, like all sales organizations, we're always balancing our focus between driving client results and meeting our revenue commitments. We take them extremely seriously and are maniacally obsessed with achieving both. For many years, I led the team that supported a $30 million channel that responded well to promotions—buy forty of these, and we'll provide you this; buy a hundred of these, and you get your choice of these three rewards. And with over a hundred salespeople in the United States, it became quite competitive, as we would incentivize their sales goals. In the sales world, it's called a SPIF (sales performance incentive fund), and most salespeople love it when they're launched.

These campaigns would usually last between ten days and three weeks. To encourage involvement (and competition) among the distributed sales team, we published a daily scoreboard that was emailed companywide, often several times a day. Now, if you're thinking a scoreboard is some isolated linear bar chart, you'd be the musical equivalent to uberconservative Perry Como (google Perry Como if you don't know who that is). What I'm talking about is on the other end of the spectrum, as in "Ozzy Osbourne biting off a bat's head" outrageous. (Every teenager in the 1980s knew this story, which amounts to the sum of my knowledge about Ozzy Osbourne, or, for that matter, bats.)

Putting my terrible music metaphors aside, I created fun, blushworthy scoreboards—lighthearted and based on a story line with the field sales team as the winners and losers that day. Typically tied to something happening in the news, they featured running themes like the Olympics, a presidential election, or some celebrity scandal we could make light of. We were always pushing the edge—sometimes too far, I admit, but they created and sustained interest and engagement. Oddly, six-figure salespeople want their heads Photoshopped on Michael Phelps's or Gabrielle Reece's body like you can't believe, especially when they're being called out for outstanding performance that day. And want to motivate the underperformers? Shame them a bit (in a respectful, playful way), and you'll find increased activity, as nobody wanted to be shamed on Scott's infamous scoreboards. For the record, I would typically give them a heads-up so they could gird their loins, so to speak, and be prepped with a witty response to their lighthearted public flogging. Our culture at

FranklinCovey might be conservative, but we all trusted each other's intent so we could have loads of fun teasing each other. Keep in mind, these outrageous scoreboards typically focused on and featured salespeople, who generally love the limelight. Any press is good press, right? No?

Obviously, every culture has different tolerances and sensitivities, and as I look back in today's culture, I could have tightened up a few references, as times have changed. But there is a direct correlation to how fun, engaging, and viral your internal scoreboards are and how they drive and track behavior. Many high-performing, serious, buttoned-down associates would tell me it was the highlight of their sometimes tedious and even lonely day to see the scoreboard show up in their inbox. They'd open it immediately to see who was being pilloried that day—or, preferably, who was being lauded by seeing their photos featured as leading out on the current campaign.

Exercise good judgment and have a diverse team that crosses multiple sectors of your firm vet what's reasonable and what's not. But, most of all, have fun and make your compelling scoreboard highly visual and accessible.

. . .

THE TRANSFORMATIONAL INSIGHT

People want to win in every part of their life—especially in their career. Provide a compelling, evergreen scoreboard that ensures clarity and builds engagement.

THE QUESTION

If it were illegal to use Excel or any bar-chart-generating software package, how would your scoreboard efforts look, track, and, more importantly, drive your desired behaviors?

DANIEL AMEN

FRANKLINCOVEY
ONLEADERSHIP
WITH SCOTT MILLER

EPISODE 8

DANIEL AMEN
PROTECT YOUR BRAIN

Let me start by saying I'm not a *complete* alarmist—especially with health issues. I wear sunscreen occasionally and I eat donuts—also occasionally. I sometimes go to the gym and I sometimes don't. I have my teeth cleaned annually, a dermatologist appointment every three or four years, and a complete physical once a year. I'm also late on my colonoscopy (I'm going . . . this year, I promise). I consume moderate amounts of alcohol, caffeine, and water, typically in that order. I've been known to eat fruits and vegetables, but I admit red and green peppers are simply a delivery device for bleu cheese dressing. Hey, I could have just put it in a spoon, so give me a little credit.

My grade is about a B– on most health issues from the neck down. From the head up, I'm an A+, thanks to Dr. Daniel Amen. And that matters because our brain function is evident in every aspect of our lives. When your prefrontal cortex is overactive, it's often the cause of interpersonal conflict, which, if left untreated, can lead to lifelong challenges. When our amygdala isn't functioning properly, we can experience anxiety and depression levels we mistakenly attribute to other pressures in life. So there are plenty of good reasons to keep the brain healthy. And as you've no doubt experienced in this book, many of the Master Mentor insights are about turning on the mind's proverbial light bulb as you see something from a new perspective. This chapter's transformational insight is less about turning the light bulb on and more about the need to protect the light bulb itself.

I am proud to say that even with three young sons—ages six, eight, and ten—we've had no broken bones or trips to the hospital (yet), but that likely comes at their fun expense because I carefully limit their adventures. Overlimit is likely more accurate. I open with this because the insight I want to share from Dr. Amen might squelch some of your own fun and adventure to ensure you protect your physical brain. I've known Dr. Amen for over a decade and have read many of his books, including my favorite, *Change Your Brain, Change Your Life*. He has dedicated most of his professional life as a psychiatrist and neuroscientist to helping people care for the one organ many experts spend virtually no time talking about, and one you can't see in most checkups. Think about this: Medical professionals can check your heart health, the function of your lungs, skin, eyes, hearing, blood pressure, and nearly every other major bodily function including your kidneys, colon, and breasts. But when was the last time, other than hearing someone suffered a "mild" concussion, you had your brain checked? At least not until Dr. Daniel Amen came on the scene as what I like to refer to as "the Dr. Oz of the brain."

Daniel Amen founded Amen Clinics and has authored dozens of bestselling books. He pushes the normal conversation about brain care and even how to treat mental illness. He's appeared on practically every television talk show highlighting brain health and is one of PBS's largest fundraisers. If your television is turned to PBS on weekends , you've likely seen him dozens of times.

I respect Dr. Amen's maniacal focus on brain health, but like all of us, I don't do my absolute best with feeding my brain. Hence the donuts and bleu cheese. (When he reads this, I guarantee I will get a call or text.) What I like most about Daniel is his motive. He cares about people's health. He genuinely and passionately wants not only his patients to live full lives—there are nine Amen Clinics in the United States—but he sincerely strives to change human habits so our lives are longer, richer, and more satisfying. Too many physicians have a standard "Let's get you on medication" approach to medicine (or with many non-MDs, they look solely to herbs and other naturopathic solutions). Daniel is an expert on both ends and every option in between, including exercise, diet, social interactions, and a litany of options carefully tailored to the individual. I've seen him counsel many friends of mine, from executives to teenagers, and when they share their experience with him, it's never the same program twice.

But the flip side of having a world-renowned neuroscientist as a personal friend is going to a restaurant with him. (Some advice: Eat before you go!) Joining Daniel for dinner is like going to High Mass with the pope. Not going to High Mass to *see* the pope, but having the pope sit in your pew *next* to you listening to you recite the prayers. Let's just say it's daunting, and he likes it that way!

But this chapter's insight is less about your diet and more about protecting your brain and the brains of those you care about from physical injury. (To be clear though, I have learned an immense amount from him about the importance of diet, exercise, mental stimulation, and the role our emotional health plays not just in maintaining good brain function, but also in decelerating the onset of diseases such as dementia and Alzheimer's.)

Dr. Amen's relentlessly evangelizing of the need for all of us to protect our brain begins on the most basic level by wearing a helmet during our now-normalized activities like football, soccer, or skateboarding. Or, in my case, because of the idiotic decision to buy my son a hoverboard. ("But, Dad, Charlie's had his for six months and hasn't fallen once!")

I don't want this insight to be a killjoy, but sometimes solid advice is. Dr. Amen is unrelenting in educating us about the extraordinarily delicate makeup of our brains. Brains that are the consistency of Jell-O. This fact alone should alarm you when you think about how you subjected your head to punishing attempts to make soccer goals when you were young, or, even worse, when watching your teenager get slammed to the ground on Friday evenings during the fall football season. (I just lost a few thousand Texan followers on Facebook and LinkedIn for that one.) And to further horrify you, our tofu-like brains are enclosed in an extremely pointy, sharp skull meant to protect it. That's like coating the family Bible in Sterno and setting it near the gas stove. Seems like a bit of a design flaw if you ask me (or, if you're sitting next to the pope, ask him).

Through interviewing Daniel, I better appreciate not just the role our brain plays in our daily functioning (because most medical focus is on our heart or other organs) but, as a father, my responsibility to protect those jelly like organs in my three sons. I have unilaterally eliminated certain sports as options, which is why you see so many social media posts about my boys playing tennis—it's one sport Daniel and I landed on that would be least likely to cause a head trauma.

Call me crazy. I don't care. I've watched close-up as friends and neighbors have had their lives forever altered (or ended) as a result of not taking some simple precautions to protect their brain. You may know that my friend and mentor, Dr. Stephen R. Covey, died because of a brain injury from a bicycle accident. (He was wearing a helmet, just not properly tightened.)

By now I'm sure you think I'm a pansy (especially if you're from Texas), but I truly had an epiphany when I listened to Dr. Amen. In his role as a psychiatrist and brain-imaging expert, Dr. Amen has scanned nearly 180,000 brains. He talks about the lifelong impact resulting from otherwise seemingly harmless activities: the junior high school tackle that results in a concerning but recoverable concussion; the dirt-bike accident that doesn't end in immediate trauma but is followed by difficulty in school, romantic relationships, and careers; the young twin who rolls out of their bunk bed and lands on their head, then years later realizes their multiple divorces, bankruptcies, and general level of interpersonal agitation was highly correlated to that untreated brain injury . . . thirty years ago.

So, should we all walk around in a helmet, eating blueberries dipped in coconut oil rolled in chia seeds?

Yes. But of course that's absurd. Unless you're my wife. But sadly, Dr. Amen is not a marriage counselor.

What we need to do is take this expert's lifework to heart and be uberdiligent about understanding how we must protect our own and our children's brains until they are old enough to understand their fragility and properly care for themselves. My boys aren't on trampolines (that's another nightmare to avoid), we wear helmets on anything with wheels, and we have an absolute blast finding joy and challenge in many sports and family activities (water balloons are a staple).

If you want to give your family, friends, and colleagues a unique gift, heighten their awareness that the person in their life—be it a spouse, a child, an in-law, or a neighbor—who may seem angry, easily irritated, incapable of forming healthy long-term relationships, or is churning through careers, may in fact have an undiagnosed or untreated brain injury. I highly recommend visiting Amenclinics.com or calling one of his clinics for a consultation. You might save a marriage. You might even save a life.

It may well be yours.

Yes, I recognize this insight is a bit of an outlier and may feel dramatic. You're welcome.

. . .

THE TRANSFORMATIONAL INSIGHT

Just because you can't see your brain doesn't mean it's not there. Invest as much energy caring for it as you do your heart, lungs, skin, and other more conspicuous organs.

THE QUESTION

Are you willing to become the family or community pariah in order to save a life? Dramatic? Yes. Accurate? Even more so.

GENERAL STANLEY MCCHRYSTAL

FRANKLINCOVEY
ONLEADERSHIP
WITH SCOTT MILLER

EPISODE 27

GENERAL STANLEY MCCHRYSTAL

BE ON THE RIGHT SIDE OF HISTORY

Being in the presence of a military leader of General McChrystal's four-star stature was a career highlight for me. This despite a family history, other than my father's time in the National Guard, lacking military service. My admiration for the people serving as guardians of our democracy and way of life couldn't be higher. It's just that I've had little firsthand exposure to the military, so I was truly honored to have General McChrystal as our guest to discuss his thoroughly pragmatic yet inspirational book *Leaders: Myth and Reality*. Now, I'll admit, I was a bit stunned General McChrystal granted us an interview at all, given his experiences with rogue interviewers. Nor am I blind to the fact that many hold strong opinions about politics, perceived American international interventionism, war, or other legitimately debatable topics that might muddle an open-mindedness toward his transformational insights. If for no other reason than his undeniable selfless service to our nation, I ask you to suspend your judgment on such matters if you fall into that category and truly lean in to this story. Robert Gates, the esteemed former secretary of defense, described General McChrystal as "perhaps the finest warrior and leader of men in combat I've ever met." Call me simple-minded, but that's good enough for me.

I came to know General McChrystal through a mutual friend, Joel Peterson, the famed Stanford University professor, author, entrepreneur, chairman of JetBlue Airways, and a member of FranklinCovey's board of directors. Joel is one of the most connected leaders I know, and only associates with people of the highest competence and character (which is why you might wonder why he's friends with me!). Prior to interviewing the general, I read *Leaders: Myth and Reality* and knew immediately which story would form this chapter's transformative insight. A bit of foreshadowing—it involves being on the right side of history.

For those of you who may have forgotten, General McChrystal retired from the United States Army after many decades of military service, culminating as commander of the United States military operations in Afghanistan in the mid-2000s. His military career ended rather abruptly when a *Rolling Stone* interview reported derogatory comments from him and his staff where they appeared to mock top civilian officials. This resulted in his resignation to then president Barack Obama and an excuse-free apology where he wrote, "I extend my sincerest apology for this profile. It was a mistake reflecting poor judgment and should never have happened. Throughout my career, I have lived by the principles of personal honor and professional integrity. What is reflected in this article falls far short of that standard."[1] You had to be living under a rock (in Afghanistan) not to recall this incident, and if you're the one human being who's never misspoken and then regretted it, go ahead and skip this chapter. For the rest of us, here comes the transformational insight.

During the first year of their marriage, General McChrystal's wife, Annie, purchased a $25 print of Robert E. Lee as a gift for him. General McChrystal had spent much of his early life admiring General Lee, had grown up near General Lee's home, and had even attended Washington-Lee High School. General McChrystal lived in Lee Barracks while attending the United States Military Academy and had, like many, put General Lee on a pedestal for his service to the military and nation. Many revered and respected Lee as a decisive and even courteous leader, including President Lincoln himself. Lincoln appointed Lee as major general and offered him command of the Union army—a command Lee ultimately turned down. Place Lee however you will in the context of history; he has been the subject of study and veneration by many—including Presidents Lincoln, Roosevelt, and Eisenhower—for his military skill and commitment to duty.

But something changed in 2017. Long before the social-justice protests and unrest of 2020, there was an event in Charlottesville, Virginia, considered despicable by most. A white supremacist rally called Unite the Right took place and included white nationalists, neo-Nazis, Klansmen, and other hate groups. There was a massive clash with counterprotesters, culminating in an avowed neo-Nazi ramming his car into a crowd of counterprotesters, killing a woman and injuring nineteen others. This event seemed to ignite a multiyear escalation in America, where centuries-old anger and pain began to surface and communities all across the nation finally confronted their own racial viewpoints. These were often symbolized in the removal of local Civil War statues, and schools and universities debating renaming various buildings. Local municipalities also faced the highly charged decisions of renaming parks and other government-owned facilities.

Shortly after this horrific incident, a month of discussion ensued where General McChrystal's wife encouraged him to take down the picture of General Robert E. Lee. Her position was that guests to their home, post Charlottesville, might misconstrue General McChrystal's support for General Lee as supporting the despicable agenda of the recent rally related to the controversy surrounding the removal of a local General Lee statue. Although General McChrystal publicly condemned the events, he spent a month deliberating his wife's counsel: he had rationalized that because it was a gift from her and had hung in every home of theirs for forty-one years, it was worth keeping.

But then, one Sunday, he took it down and walked it to the trash.

Now you might wonder why it took him so long to remove it from the wall. Others might ask why a potential US presidential candidate like General McChrystal was so supportive of another general who led the fight to keep slaves during the Civil War. Any of us who have studied General Lee know him to be a very complicated character, much like many of the presidents we revere before him and since. I'm quite certain General McChrystal, if given a platform, could school many of us on US history and the honorable military career General Lee and others of his time served. That's in no way a defense of General Lee or any Americans involved in the grotesque history of slavery as the transformational insight in this chapter will soon illustrate.

Let's agree to put that assessment aside for another book.

Earlier, I wrote about being on the right side of history. This is usually a term reserved for members of the Supreme Court, presidents, senators, members of Congress, or other nationally elected officials. This might not be worthy of inclusion had General McChrystal taken it down in the summer of 2020. We all learned a lot in a period of a few weeks following the death of George Floyd and other black Americans. It was these moments that horrifically caught the attention of the world and represented the long struggle championed by Dr. Martin Luther King and others before him and since. Personally, as a white man in my fifties, it was the first time I deeply contemplated the meaning of Black Lives Matter. I also came to understand and appreciate what white privilege means and not to be offended by it but rather become introspective around it. And so many other lessons that came through dialogue with like-minded and not-so-like-minded friends, family, neighbors, and even business colleagues. But the point of this chapter is that, three years prior to that moment, General McChrystal, in a quiet act of integrity, in the privacy of his own family and home, made a decision and took action. He reversed his own long-entrenched point of view and changed his mind. His perspective evolved and he accepted a new reality. And he did it not because of a large social movement taking form around him, but because his wife reminded him what the painting had come to mean—something that stood apart from who General McChrystal was and what he valued. This is what being on the right side of history is all about—recognizing a visible incongruence and standing up for the greater good, even if it means challenging, evolving, or simply letting go of once-cherished beliefs. Sometimes such choices are easy, but often they are not.

Being on the right side of history is a leadership competency and requires leaders to be willing and capable of changing their mind—not so willy-nilly that their brand waffles and aligns with the last argument or position they were exposed to, but genuinely, thoughtfully, and deliberately considering opposing viewpoints. It requires a healthy dose of both confidence and humility, often trading short-term gains for long-term wins on matters small and large, both private and public.

When someone steps up to the challenge of being on the right side of history, their example ends up as a model for others. Team members who see their leaders demonstrate this in the face of new facts, cultural shifts, and critical inflection points will be more empowered to do the same.

I'd suggest each of us use the standard to further consider our own political and social positions, as well as the decisions we make as formal leaders inside organizations, members of social clubs, and religious institutions—really, every role we play in life. Are we able to take a step back, move off our entrenched positions and beliefs (many deeply inculcated), and exercise more compassion, humility, and humanity for others? Changing your mind and taking a stand on the right side of history will always be a sign of strength and never a weakness. I find it powerfully motivating that a man like General McChrystal, with so many accomplishments across a storied military career, could inspire me most by a simple act of integrity done privately and quietly in his own home.

Another example comes to mind, involving one of the world's most renowned and influential publishing houses, Simon & Schuster. Recently, its renowned and respected CEO, Carolyn Reidy, passed away after years in that role. Her colleague Jonathan Karp was promoted to the CEO position, and in short order announced the hiring of an external candidate to become the new senior vice president and publisher. Dana Canedy, perhaps best known as the administrator of the Pulitzer Prizes, joined Simon & Schuster after several years of Jonathan's unsuccessful professional overtures to her. As reported in the *New York Times*, Dana addresses the timing of becoming the third woman and first Black person to hold the position: "Jon should get credit for the fact that in an era of racial reckoning, when suddenly everybody is looking for people of color and women to add to their boards and to bring in to their companies—he started talking to me two years ago. . . . That's the way you want to go into a company. I wouldn't be taking this job if I thought he just wanted a Black publisher."[2]

I've highlighted this example of Jonathan Karp "being on the right side of history" because, although Simon & Schuster isn't the publisher of this particular book, he and his associates have set a superb example for all leaders and industries. Like General

McChrystal, he acted based on principles and not just peer pressure or what's currently popular and in vogue in society. For those of you thinking that both could have acted sooner, we can all benefit from the Chinese proverb: "The best time to plant a tree was twenty years ago. The second-best time is now."

. . .

THE TRANSFORMATIONAL INSIGHT

You are leaving a historical legacy, whether you're conscious of it or not. Make the choice to be on the right side of history now before you're forced to be a casualty on the other side later.

THE QUESTION

If a historian were chronicling your decisions, what might you pause and do differently?

KIM SCOTT

FRANKLINCOVEY
ONLEADERSHIP
WITH SCOTT MILLER

EPISODE 58

KIM SCOTT
RADICAL CANDOR

Ever read a book and think, *This is my book; I was supposed to write this book*! For me, it was *Radical Candor* by Kim Scott. It's an absolute masterpiece that took four years to draft, and draws on her own impressive career at multiple failed startups and her significant roles at both Google and Apple.

Sometimes in life a colleague recommends a book to you, and you're not sure if they think you need it for improvement or validation. I'm pleased to report that my friend and FranklinCovey colleague James McDermott saw Kim speak at a conference, bought me a copy the same day, drove it to my home, and told me I absolutely had to read the book. Fortunately, he clarified as he handed it to me, it was a book I'd love because it spoke to my unique brand of leadership. Being handed a book as a compliment and not as a prescription for fixing something likely only happens once in your career. Hopefully, your book reading list is growing from all my recommendations. Now add to it *Radical Candor: Be a Kickass Boss Without Losing Your Humanity*. It's a compulsory read for every leader of people.

Kim learned early in her career—working, oddly enough, with Russian diamond cutters—that leadership is "giving a damn about the people you work with." It could have been said more gently perhaps, but Kim's book isn't titled *Delicate Candor* either. Conversely, Kim has dedicated her career to helping teach leaders the value of Radical Candor—a style of leadership and communication that can transform people's self-awareness and the performance of entire teams and cultures. It's caring about the people you work with on a deep, personal level, being willing to challenge them directly when necessary, and having real human relationships at work.

This is the life's work of our own cofounder Dr. Stephen R. Covey and his eldest son, Stephen M. R. Covey, who promotes in his own seminal book, *The Speed of Trust: The One Thing That Changes Everything*, that the greatest gift a leader can give their team members is feedback on their blind spots.

Kim believes too many leaders want to be "nice" to their employees and ensure they don't "hurt their feelings." As a result, they take this sentiment way too far in the culture they model and build. For fear of offending an employee, they shy away from confronting certain behaviors and results. As a consequence, they demoralize their top performers, who often quit as a result. This is a vicious cycle that repeats itself across teams globally every day. And it's 100 percent the leader's fault and responsibility to change. Or another thing happens—they don't give poor performers the opportunity to improve and wind up having to fire them. Not so nice after all. In this scenario, the leader most certainly missed ample opportunities to hold specific, high-courage, Radical Candor conversations that could have saved the employee's job and even altered the trajectory of their future career. Through building their self-awareness and ensuring the team member is clear on what success looks like for them, lives and livelihoods can be altered for the better.

I would add that leaders rarely love their employees enough to risk not being liked. Read that line twice—there may be some lessons in it for you.

I've never heard a better example of this than the story Kim shares of an experience she had when she worked for Sheryl Sandberg at Google. In fact, it's so valuable that, with Kim's permission, I have inserted the transcript from our podcast interview. I prefer Kim tell you the story in exactly her own words, so hold on for this ride:

> SCOTT MILLER: I feel like I've met my leadership muse in Kim Scott. Kim, you share a great story early on about an encounter you had—I think it was with your boss and Larry Page at Google. And it was kind of instructive to your understanding the necessity and the value, the pricelessness, of letting the most senior person model this concept and how it changes the culture. Take your time and walk us through that story, because I think there's such great leadership currency in it.
>
> KIM SCOTT: So, shortly after I joined Google, I had to give a presentation to the founders and the CEO about how the AdSense business was doing. And I walked into the room and there is Sergey Brin, one of the founders, on an elliptical trainer and toe shoes in one corner of the room, pedaling away or stepping away. And in the other corner of the room is Eric Schmidt, who was Google's CEO at the time, and he was so deep in his email, it was like his brain had been plugged into his machine. And like any normal person in this situation, I felt a little bit nervous. How in the world was I supposed to get

these people's attention? Luckily for me, the AdSense business was on fire. And when I said how many new customers had joined in the previous two weeks, Eric almost fell off his chair. He said, "What did you say? This is incredible. What do you need? Do you need more marketing dollars? Do you need more engineers? How can we help you keep this business miracle going?" So I'm feeling like the meeting's going okay. In fact, I now believe I'm a genius. And I walked out the door.

I walked past my boss, who was Sheryl Sandberg. And I'm expecting a high five, a pat on the back or something. And instead, Sheryl says to me, "Why don't you walk back to my office with me?" And I thought, oh, gosh, I screwed something up. And I'm sure I'm about to hear about it. Sheryl began the conversation by telling me about the things that had gone well in the meeting. Not in the "feedback sandwich" sense of the word—the sort of kiss me, kick me, kiss me style . . . I always get that phrase wrong.

But of course, all I wanted to know was what I had done wrong. And eventually, Sheryl said to me, "You said 'um' a lot in there. Were you aware of it?"

I made this kind of brush-off gesture with my hand. I said, "Yeah, it's a verbal tic. No big deal, really."

And then she said, "I know this great speech coach. I bet that Google would pay for it. Would you like an introduction?"

Once again, I sort of made this brush-off gesture with my hand and I said, "No, I'm busy. Didn't you hear about all these new customers we have? I don't have time for a speech coach."

Then Sheryl stopped. She looked me right in the eye and she said, "I can see when you do that thing with your hand that I'm going to have to be a lot more direct with you. When you say 'um' every third word, it makes you sound stupid."

Now she's got my full attention. And some people would say it was mean of Sheryl to say I sounded stupid, but in fact, it was the kindest thing she could have done for me at the moment, because if she hadn't used just those words with me (and she wouldn't have used them with other people on her team who were better listeners than I was), then I wouldn't have gone to see the speech coach, and I wouldn't have realized she was not exaggerating. I literally said 'um' every third word, and this was news to me, because I had been giving presentations for my entire career. In fact, I had raised money for two startups giving presentations. I thought I was pretty good at it. And this really got me to thinking—why had no one told me? It was almost as though I'd been walking through my entire career with a giant hunk of spinach between my teeth, and nobody had the common courtesy to tell me it was there. I could eliminate it if I knew about it. And so I thought, what was it about Sheryl that made it so seemingly easy for her to tell me, but also perhaps more interestingly, why had no one else told me? And I realized in the case of Sheryl, it boiled down to two things: She cared about me at a very human level, not as an employee, but as a human being. And second, she challenged me directly.

When I had a family member fall ill, she said, "I'm going to write your coverage plan. You go to the airport, get on the airplane. We've got your back." That's what teams do for each other. And that was not the kind of thing, of course, she could do for all five thousand people in her organization. But it was the kind of thing she could do for the people who worked directly with her. And that was really important because it sort of had a ripple effect. But she'll never let her concern for not hurting our feelings in the short term get in the way of her ability to challenge us directly, to tell us when we screwed up. And so it seems really simple: care personally; challenge directly.

I spent one summer at the consulting firm McKinsey. And in that summer—it was the summer between my two years at business school—I learned one really important thing: all of life's hardest problems can be boiled down to a good two-by-two framework (see Figure 1). So if you turn *care personally* and *challenge directly* into a two-by-two grid, when you care personally and challenge directly at the same time, it's radical candor. When you challenge directly, but you fail to show that you care personally, I call it *obnoxious aggression*. And I used to call that, by the way, the asshole quadrant. But I stopped doing that, and I stopped doing it for a very important reason. As soon as I did that, people would use the framework to sort of judge others and judge themselves. They'd start writing names in boxes. And I beg of you, please don't do that! The point of this framework is to use it like a compass, not like a personality test. It's not another Myers-Briggs score. Use it like a compass to guide individual conversations to a better place. So that's obnoxious aggression. Now, very often, when we realize we've been kind of a jerk, instead of moving the right way on the *care personally* dimension, we move the wrong way on *challenge directly* and we wind up in *manipulative insincerity*—the worst place of all, where you're neither caring nor challenging. That's the false apology, backstabbing behavior, that sort of thing. And those are the kinds of things we love to talk about. We love to talk about our obnoxious-aggression stories and our manipulative-insincerity stories when people have done that to us at work. But the fact of the matter is, the vast majority of people make the vast majority of their mistakes in this last quadrant where they do show they care personally, but they fail to challenge directly—usually, just because they don't want to hurt somebody's feelings. And this last quadrant I call *ruinous empathy*. And that is the thing that the book *Radical Candor* is really directed at solving because it is the most common problem.

FIGURE 1

Okay, it's Scott again. If you took any value from this passage (and if you didn't, you should probably go back and reread it), go buy *Radical Candor*. It will change your leadership brand forever.

Looking back on my own thirty-year career, the biggest pivot points in my maturity and professional progression have come when a courageous leader came to me and spoke with uncharacteristic directness and clarity about specific self-defeating behaviors I was demonstrating. Horrifying in the moment, but invaluable over time. I'll bet if you reflect on your own career, you will acknowledge the same experience. As I've said previously, the greatest leaders are those who love their employees enough to risk not being liked—at least in the moment.

. . .

THE TRANSFORMATIONAL INSIGHT

As a leader, move outside your comfort zone and discuss the undiscussables with your team members. Solicit feedback from them and give feedback in return. It's likely the greatest professional gift they'll ever receive.

THE QUESTION

How can you better recognize the blind spots of those around you, and with a balance of courage and consideration, provide them feedback for improvement? And further, how can you become more aware of your own blind spots and accept feedback from others on them?

DORIE CLARK

FRANKLINCOVEY
ONLEADERSHIP
WITH SCOTT MILLER

EPISODE 39

DORIE CLARK

TWIST IF YOU CAN'T INVENT (AND EVEN IF YOU CAN)

THE EIGHTIES WERE some of the best years for television advertising, and iconic quotes became part of everyone's lexicon: *Where's the beef? I've fallen and I can't get up. Time to make the donuts.* My favorite, though, is Smith Barney: *They make money the old-fashioned way—they earn it.*

The Smith Barney adage reminds me of Dorie Clark. Regarding her influence and following, she earned it the old-fashioned way: hard work and relentless persistence. Not that all the mentors featured here didn't do the same; I simply think it best describes Dorie's brand and impact. I know of too many "thought leaders" who've bought their way to two million LinkedIn followers or "offshored" their Facebook likes and engagement. Dorie's influence and social following has grown steadily day after day from her valuable contributions: *HBR* articles, podcast interviews, blog posts, books, assessments, newsletters, webinars, and

LinkedIn Learning videos. (For the record, I'm an avid follower and posse member, and you should be too.)

I've observed Dorie's career for years and I've partially patterned my own after hers (obviously, not yet as successfully). Some background for those who may not yet fully appreciate her journey: Dorie launched as a political reporter and then became press secretary for former US secretary of labor Robert Reich on his campaign to become governor of Massachusetts. She went on to be campaign spokesperson for former Vermont governor Howard Dean's 2004 effort to become the Democratic presidential nominee. That went well—very well, in fact, until the infamous "Dean Scream" the night of the Iowa caucuses. When the Dean campaign ended a few states later, she honed her consulting skills and began writing books about brand and marketing. She is now a renowned consultant, bestselling author, and speaker. And, perhaps most importantly, she is the very definition of what Malcolm Gladwell calls a *Connector* in his seminal book *The Tipping Point.* As Gladwell writes, Connectors are the people who "link us up with the world . . . who introduce us to our social circles . . . [who have] a special gift for bringing the world together."[1] Increasingly, many roads don't lead *to*, but *through,* Dorie Clark.

Dorie's expertise in personal reinvention and breaking through with your own brand led to her books *Reinventing You, Entrepreneurial You*, and *Stand Out*. During our *On Leadership* interview, a key concept sprung out at me. It not only immediately validated me, but I knew I'd write about it someday (welcome to someday). This wasn't Dorie's intention, but she gave me permission to copy. And when I say copy, I mean change, twist, improve, or innovate on an existing idea. This was the transformational insight she shared.

Leaders are often called on to be inventive, but I think many of us find the act of invention daunting. *Only geniuses invent, right? Engineers invent. Scientists invent. I'm not any of those, so I can't and don't invent.* Dorie's words immediately changed my mindset and she liberated me from my legacy thinking. She suggests that we release ourselves from the burden of the paralyzing overwhelm of invention. Instead, figure out a twist on a current product or idea that could dramatically change access, usage, relevance, viability, and profit for something already in the market.

I'm guessing at this point in the book, you must think I'm a Luddite. (Just the use of the word *Luddite* should shame you out of that.) "Oh, don't invent, but instead just improve . . . thanks for the transformational insight, Scott. Is that really what this chapter is about?"

Yes, you Luddite!

Here's a fairly nonlinear example of how some people may have gone about buying a dress or gown for a wedding or charity event. Forty years ago, you might have traipsed to Neiman Marcus for the ritual of the "presentation." Rounds and rounds of dresses would be brought out for preview, and the process was as much about the status of socializing (over the included lunch) as it was about a purchase. Next, enter Bloomingdale's, who brought similar fashion to the masses. Then, Nordstrom Rack, which disrupted the industry by recycling their own nonsold goods to themselves, instead of wholesaling them out to Marshalls, TJ Maxx, and Tuesday Morning. Talk about a massive "twist" in the fashion industry.

Then everything turned on its head when The RealReal and Poshmark began offering the resale of consigned luxury goods. That seemed like a game changer for "absolute necessities" like Chanel, Gucci, and Louis Vuitton, until Rent the Runway shook it all up with the same goods, but with a subscription service. This allowed consumers to change up their outfits, purses, and even high-end jewelry on a nearly nonstop basis. Then there's Trunk Club and Stitch Fix offering monthly subscription access to curated choices based on your taste and preferences. India Hicks home parties, Beauty Counter direct sales . . . it's now endless.

Say hello to the contributing causes of Neiman Marcus's recent bankruptcy. The market became irreparably fractured with new segmentations, robust channels, value propositions, and customizations. I'm captivated to see what's next. Now, you might ask, how does a fifty-three-year-old man know about all of this? Allow me to introduce you to my wife, Stephanie Miller—a savvy user of most if not all of these retailers (UPS and FedEx probably have cargo jets named in her honor). This string of industry inventions wasn't about starting from scratch. Each added to the series of twists, expanding the marketplace and creating many millionaires.

Consider the rise of Airbnb. Fifty-six years after Kemmons Wilson built the first Holiday Inn in Memphis, Tennessee, Airbnb put a fresh twist on the hospitality business. With a formula for equal parts technology and trust, the San Francisco startup has grown to over thirteen thousand employees and has hosted over 400 million guests around the world. Their twist on an old idea has completely disrupted the online-accommodations industry. Furthermore, their response to the COVID-19 pandemic and subsequent self-disruption has made them as relevant as ever and perhaps poised for even greater growth in the future.

I find Dorie's encouragement the right creative laxative for ideas stubbornly constipated in our heads. Sorry (not sorry) for that visual, but it reminds me of a time when I was living in Chicago and started a side hustle. Back around 2005, I twisted travel, currency, and jewelry into a unique and growing business. I'd seen a woman wearing Italian lira coins as earrings and thought it was a cool idea. When I asked her about them, she waxed nostalgic about her husband, their romantic trip to Italy, and the repurposed coins. I got more than I bargained for in the details, but it was the passion with which she described her Italian experience and watching her touch both earrings the entire time that sparked a desire to dig deeper. She was finding genuine enjoyment from the two now valueless (thanks to the euro) coins, and it seemed to me there was an opportunity to be had. I tried to extricate myself from the protracted descriptions of vacation stops and food reminiscing, and was half-tempted to put her on a plane back to Italy, but that seemed like overkill.

Over the next several days, I researched coin-based jewelry late into the evenings—probably the only single guy doing so in Chicago. But I found many businesses offering coin earrings, necklaces, rings, and bracelets—jewelry that included everything from ancient Greek coins for many thousands of dollars to a line of necklaces featuring each of the fifty state quarters. Tacky, perhaps, but that was someone's own twist. Then, after recounting the *twenty-minute* conversation with my Italian-vacationing friend (I kid you not), I developed an idea—truly, my twist on all I'd seen in the market. What if I could harness the passion of this lady, and countless others like her, but multiply the revenue opportunity, and profit, by capitalizing on not just her love of Italy, but *all* of her travels? (There were more vacations I'd gotten an earful about too.) So I launched a coin charm-bracelet business. But here's to Dorie's twist: not a static bracelet featuring "off the shelf" coins selected by me, but a customized collection of coins from countries of your own travel. Or your travel wish list. Or your countries of heritage. Hell, I didn't care why you wanted the coins, so long as you bought them from me.

Bam! House in the Hamptons, here I come!

I mentally envisioned every cruise line in the world carrying my custom-coin charm bracelets in their gift shops. Just finished your seven-countries-in-six-days cruise of a lifetime? Don't blow your $200 in the casino—buy my bracelet to remember your nightly mai tais and crab claws. I pictured grandmothers wearing them as Mother's Day gifts, college-bound girls exploring Europe during their gap years and buying them as keepsakes, and the perfect mother-in-law-who-has-everything gift. I nam d the business The World on Your Wrist, and set about sourcing coins. Sort of like when Germany invaded Russia thinking: *No problem, this will be a slam dunk!*

My coin sourcing grew to become a significant endeavor, as I had to learn currency values, which coins were even available for purchase in bulk, and which were high in visual appeal but low in cost. Recognizing that you can't buy in-circulation money at a discount (so any dreams of an improvement in my cost of goods was a goner), and after supply-chain struggles, hours hand-setting and customizing sterling-silver bezels, and dealing with customers who were confused about whether they went to St. Thomas or St. John or were disappointed to learn the currency is the same in England as in Scotland, it eventually ended. As overwhelming as it all was, trying to cash-flow the business toward growth without investors was more than I was willing to do, despite the business beginning to actually take off.

So I stopped. But here's the thing . . . I still consider the experience to have been massively successful—even though I lost $50,000 on the final balance sheet and never went house-hunting in the Hamptons. What I gained was the insight that I could successfully twist an existing idea into a viable business, which has given me the confidence to continue twisting and innovating in other entrepreneurial ventures. Including this very book, as I've studied the expertise and acumen of thirty people and am now applying my own twists on their original insights. And you thought you had to think up original ideas to write a book? Not so—for you, me, or anyone else. You just need a twist.

. . .

THE TRANSFORMATIONAL INSIGHT

Not only is there no shame in twisting an original idea, there is tremendous value. In many cases, it will be better accepted in the marketplace than the original version.

THE QUESTION

Can you stop questioning your lack of genius and creativity, and instead focus your ability to twist an existing idea to fill or create a new niche opportunity?

BONUS QUESTION

Would you like to buy a discounted bracelet featuring coins from such high-demand travel destinations as Iran, North Korea, or Syria? If so, I know a guy . . .

BOB WHITMAN

FRANKLINCOVEY
ONLEADERSHIP
WITH SCOTT MILLER

EPISODE 52

BOB WHITMAN
THE SERVANT LEADER

YOU'D THINK AFTER thirty years in the leadership-development industry, I'd be able to define servant leadership with crystal clarity. There are numerous books about it, and I suspect we all have a slightly different idea of what it means to be on the receiving side of it. However, like most profound things, it's more powerful when experienced. To that end, this transformational insight is about recognizing servant leadership is a choice that's within all of us, regardless of our organizational level.

Bob Whitman was a personal friend of Dr. Stephen R. Covey and served on the board of Covey's private company. A few years after the merger of Franklin Quest and Covey Leadership Center, he became the chairman and CEO of the combined companies now known as FranklinCovey. The average tenure of a CEO leading a large cap company is about five years. My sense is it might be slightly longer for mid- to small-cap companies—maybe more like seven or eight years. Bob has remained our

CEO for twenty-three years—and not because he didn't have other options. Prior to accepting the CEO position, he was on track to rival some of the greatest names in private equity. Instead, Bob stayed to right the ship (which he did), put it on the correct path forward (which he also did), and build the solutions clients need and value to ensure that its long-term position and influence in the market is robust (which he has.)

Bob was forty-four at the time he accepted the role and already had substantial experience in hospitality (hotel, dining, and resort attractions), senior housing, and commercial real estate development. He will never tell you that he graduated with his MBA from Harvard, or that he climbed the Matterhorn, or that he's taken part in the Kona Ironman more than twenty times. He will also not tell you that he's been married for more than forty years to his wife, Wendy, but my sense is that's what he's justifiably most proud of in his life.

Bob's been extraordinarily successful in life. Not without some setbacks like us all, but his overall batting average is quite extraordinary. He sets his mind to accomplish something and nothing stops him. I suspect he's earned some financial rewards along the way as well. Or, as my three sons who know Bob like to say, "Dad, Bob's got some serious coin!"

A scan through my several books will show that Bob has played a role in all of them, either directly or indirectly. The fact that I've selected him as a Master Mentor is both nonpolitical and (if you're read my other books) probably not all that surprising. For those Machiavellian skeptics out there, please note I'm well past the point of sucking up to the boss, I don't shy from controversy, and I have little fear of getting canned. I've always believed that the best day of your career is getting hired; the second-best day is when you're fired. So anyone I've selected as a Master Mentor has been solely included because they've earned it. At least in my mind, anyway. And since it's my book, that's the mind that counts the most.

As our insight in this chapter is servant leadership, I'd like to mention two stories about Bob that he probably doesn't even remember and would completely deny if he did. One of my critiques of Bob would be that I think he shows too much humility. To be fair, he'd likely say I show too little. On this point, we're both right.

Example One: It was 2004 and I was working in Chicago as the managing director of our Central Region. I was leading sales for the largest geographic area for our company, and we were about to host our annual regional sales meeting. Not massive—about fifty associates typically, but this year, Bob was trying to build better synergies between our two company divisions so the event size grew significantly. At the time, we still had close to 170 retail stores servicing individual consumers with productivity tools (B2C) complemented by our organizational consulting services (B2B), and we were looking at ways to collaborate and lift both divisions. The entire B2C business was successfully divested about two years later when it became clear the future of the firm globally was to pursue a focus on organizational performance and serve individuals through their employers.

At this particular sales meeting, we invited about 120 associates from both divisions in the Central Region, and for the first time met together for several days to strategize. This required a good deal of logistical planning, agenda-item debating, and team-building designing.

On the first day of the conference, at about 11:15 a.m., I stepped out of the ballroom to check on the lunch buffet to ensure it was all set and ready to push everyone through in seventy-five minutes (yes, the trains ran on time in my division) and we were all ready to go. At 11:25, just as we were breaking, the hotel fire alarm rang. A fire drill in the middle of our annual event? Come on, people!

Everyone sauntered outside (it's always interesting to see how casually adults exit buildings when alarms are sounding), and we all congregated in the parking lot. It was late September, so the weather wasn't an issue as we all stood around and chatted. About ten fire trucks rolled in and we started to see smoke coming out of the top of the hotel. Turns out an air-conditioning system had malfunctioned and there was a serious but immediately contained meltdown going on with some rooftop compressors.

Fast-forward about forty-five minutes, and we're all still standing in the parking lot trying to assess what's likely to happen next. Periodic updates from the hotel team were helpful yet inconclusive, and people weren't just getting hungry, the clock was ticking on our event. (We'd flown about 80 of the 120 associates in for two days, and this wasn't a small investment for us.)

Soon it was closing in on 1:00 p.m., and we couldn't bring the buffet to the parking lot—I know this because I tried. And it's not an option to just skip lunch either (something I covered with Dan Pink in chapter five). So, as I'm the local host, Bob and I continued to talk about options. I glanced at the pizza parlor across the road, which, candidly, I'd been thinking about as a backup for the last thirty minutes. I walked over to Bob, suggested the new pizza plan, and in two seconds he agreed. I dashed over to scope out the capacity, asked the owners if they could accommodate 120 people, and soon the famished, fatigued, and fire-weary group headed over. My assistant Ginette and I got all the attendees seated, more or less filling the place.

It's worth noting that I didn't report directly to Bob—I was a managing director reporting to a vice president, who reported to a divisional president, who reported to Bob as the CEO. And the same structure was represented from the other division as well. So, including me, there were six senior leaders at the event—seven with Bob. Suddenly, the room felt more like we'd stepped into a Medieval Times restaurant as our conference attendees (both leaders and associates) held knives and forks upright and seemed ready to pound on the tables and demand turkey legs! Not that I had time to think much about it; as the host, I went to the counter and started ordering pizzas while juggling a barrage of incoming texts with various dietary restrictions and preferences. Then, to my surprise, I caught sight of Bob and Ginette running pitchers of soda to the thirty tables. Before long, Bob was back at the counter with me, making sure I'd ordered enough, and then ran shakers of red pepper flakes and Parmesan to all the tables. As salads, cheese sticks, and stuffed mushrooms appeared in record speed, I saw Bob moving from table to table effortlessly serving everyone. I actually saw someone ask the CEO for a root beer refill. What the . . . ?

Sixty pizzas started coming, and forty minutes later, Bob was still running food with Ginette and me to the entire team. He never stopped for a drink or to eat. What I recall most about the pizza-recovery experience was not the request for the CEO to refill someone's root-beer pitcher, but seeing Bob serve the group of vice presidents and presidents, who were kind of clueless about what it was taking to support this hungry mob so we could get back to the meeting and accomplish some of the goals we'd agreed to achieve.

Was all of this for show with Bob simply playing the role of martyr? Nope. It's just who he is. Bob's a servant leader, literally and metaphorically. Nor was this an outlier—it's how he thinks. Bob is one of the most well-educated, disciplined, gracious, deliberate, and indefatigably hardworking leaders I know. At that point in his career, he deserved to be sitting and chatting up his leadership team, waiting for some invisible server or junior staff member to deliver a slice. But the exact opposite happened. Plus, Bob's not petty like me and didn't even notice the senior leaders all sitting down waiting to be served. Or maybe he's just more of a gentleman and chose to ignore it and not write about it in a book fifteen years later. Either way, it's called servant leadership.

Example Two: A few years before the pizza scenario, I found myself at Bob's second home in Dallas, Texas. Bob had moved from

Texas to Utah to assume the CEO role and kept his Dallas home, which was on a lake and came complete with a ski boat, jet skis, and a game room worthy of MTV's newest series, *Sick CEO Cribs*.

Bob had invited about ten of the senior sales leaders for a two-day strategy meeting. On the morning of the first day, I woke up early and quietly entered the kitchen around 6:00 a.m. To my surprise, Bob was there, showered and dressed for the day of meetings, and in the midst of making bacon and eggs for ten-plus people. He'd also made coffee, had orange juice poured, and was crouched down and going through the cupboards. It's then that I noticed he was on the phone with someone back in Utah, whispering to them that he couldn't find something. Bob's family employs a chef to help organize meals for a large family, many holiday celebrations, and a seemingly endless roster of business meetings hosted at his home. This is who he was on the phone with and was asking her where the chargers were. Well, for those of you who skipped cotillion in junior high, chargers are the decorative, oversized plates placed under your actual dining plate when entertaining. Not only was Bob making breakfast for his employees, he was calling his chef (a time zone earlier) to ensure the settings were perfect. Bob needed to locate the chargers. Duh!

Again, this wasn't Bob showing off his home (although it was spectacular) or trying to impress his team with dishes and his culinary skills. Bob just wanted people to feel special, cared about, and loved. Bob doesn't cut corners. Not on refilling root beer. Not on chargers. Not on the company P&L. Bob models both the character and competence he wants to see in others. He truly loves those who work at FranklinCovey, and it shows. It's not lip service at a town hall meeting or the requisite pablum in the annual report. It's the behavior behind the words, best experienced in unexpected moments, that becomes a learning opportunity for the rest of your life. It is servant leadership at its literal best.

. . .

THE TRANSFORMATIONAL INSIGHT

Servant leadership doesn't always literally mean serving. But sometimes it does.

THE QUESTION

How would you define and model servant leadership in every role of your life: parent, spouse, leader, colleague, committee member, and so on?

SUSAN CAIN

FRANKLINCOVEY
ONLEADERSHIP
WITH SCOTT MILLER

EPISODE 2

SUSAN CAIN
RETHINKING INTROVERTS AND EXTROVERTS

The Master Mentor for this chapter is Susan Cain, so pardon a small detour before I get to her brilliance. I have a brother named Michael Miller and we look nearly identical. Same height, hair, eyes, and square chin. It's quite remarkable, given a nearly four-year difference, so much so that people still stop us in restaurants and ask if we're twins.

Other than identical physical features, we share little else in common. Mike is a chemical engineer, master black belt, Six Sigma expert, and earned a double MS degree in business and chemical engineering from MIT. He was one of only forty-five students each year that are admitted to the Sloan School of Business on a full scholarship known as Leaders for Global Operations. This program is funded through investments from several dozen global companies looking to develop the next generation of technical leaders from one of the finest engineering schools in the world. And his career is a testament to the program, as he is the former CEO of two Amazon-owned companies and has held C-level positions at several other well-known brands. The guy is a remarkably talented executive-level leader.

Mike is rather reserved, shy even. Although he can manage to hold his own in any social setting, it's clearly not his preferred element, and I suspect he's relieved when he can leave most large social gatherings.

Then there's me. While my brother was memorizing Latin flashcards in high school (resulting in a Latin-based scholarship to college) I was . . . doing something so unmemorable, I can't even remember.

I left high school both Latin and scholarship-free, and entered community college. After ten years, I scraped by with the easiest education achievable: organizational communications from a liberal-arts college. But before you feel too sorry for me, I do have my own set of skills. I worked as hard as my genius brother and, as you know, am privileged to host the world's largest weekly leadership podcast for FranklinCovey. I am also honored to speak on stages around the world to thousands of people based on several of my own bestselling books. I couldn't explain lean manufacturing if my life depended on it, but give me a microphone and put me onstage in front of thousands of people to speak about my passions and I'm guaranteed to crush it.

Simply put, Mike's an introvert and I'm an extrovert. And we're both, by many comparisons (except by our parents) very successful. Oh, trust me, they think *he's* successful!

Enter Susan Cain and her remarkable book *Quiet: The Power of Introverts in a World That Can't Stop Talking*—a book my brother has read twice because of its validating premise.

Although Susan was the second interview to air on our podcast, she was actually the first interview I taped. To that point, I both thank her for being so gracious and patient and apologize for my novice interviewing skills. Fortunately, my lack of expertise did not diminish any of hers. That said, it is amusing to note that Scott Miller interviewing Susan Cain is like the chairperson of the Republican National Committee interviewing the chairperson of the Democratic National Committee. It was viscerally obvious that I'm a raging extrovert and Susan is . . . well, let's just say *not*. The fact that her husband is a self-acknowledged extrovert says a lot about Susan's view that the world benefits from all kinds of temperaments. Even so, I joked that my version of her book would have been titled: *Loud: The Power of Extroverts in a World Where Some Are Frustratingly Not.*

The transformational insight from our conversation and her book is one of those duh moments. People are different from me, and I need to not only respect that but also honor and learn from them to accelerate my own maturity. This requires us to move outside of our comfort zones and recognize that many of us fall into the time-honored rut that "people like people like themselves." And as Susan brings to life so adeptly in her book *Quiet*, introverts are often fighting upstream against a torrent of extroverts to have their ideas, creativity, and genius heard. Candidly, its extroverts like me who tend to drown them out. After reading Susan's book and interviewing her, I became much more aware of the *tsunami* that is Scott Miller and what it must be like to work for or with someone like me. Probably energy-infusing for fellow extroverts. Probably energy-depleting for introverts. As Susan writes, "We live with a value system that I call the *extrovert ideal*—the omnipresent belief that the ideal self is gregarious, alpha, and comfortable in the spotlight. . . . Introversion—along with its cousins sensitivity, seriousness, and shyness—is now a second-class personality trait, somewhere between a disappointment and a pathology."[1] I've come to understand that I partially bought in to such assessments, and my leadership style likely reflected it.

So, what can an extrovert learn from an introvert?

"Sam" was a savvy and resilient salesperson I once led and someone I would define as an introvert. That style generally frustrated me, as I was under the impression that to be an effective salesperson, you needed to be outwardly charismatic. A connector. A networker. Great salespeople were "people" people. They commanded attention from others, led the pace of conversations, and dominated opinions because they lived by a "lead or be led" mantra. (Okay, so I was an idiot, but hang in there with me . . . this was some years ago.)

Sam and I couldn't have been more different. But sadly, perhaps for him, I was the boss, and like many fear-based cultures in which I had some practical knowledge, team members typically assimilate more toward the leader's style than the other way around. I'm not sure Sam did either, but I do recall with piercing detail one meeting where our styles clashed, and the outcome was a significant learning lesson for me. Embarrassingly, many years later.

At the time, I was leading sales for a fifteen-state area. Typically, once or twice a year, I would gather the entire sales team for a day or two of strategy and skill development. I recall one such meeting where I was in classic Scott Miller leadership mode (translation: I will wear you down until you eventually agree with me . . . or at least fake it enough to convince me I've won you over). Sadly, my wife does not think this is, in fact, an asset of mine but rather a glaring liability.

Okay, back to the meeting. I'd just finished my predictable soliloquy, when it was time for questions and answers from the broader group. I can't even recall the agenda item, but suffice it to say, it was likely a change in strategy that would require all of us to shift our mindsets and behaviors. Not always desirable, but absolutely necessary to thrive, especially in a sales role. I recall poignantly watching Sam through the entire meeting. He didn't say a word. No questions. No comments. Not a supportive or dissenting remark. Zilch. To my credit and his likely delight, I don't think I pressed him as I was busy fielding questions, comments, roadblocks, and absorbing the few ass-kissing compliments from the sycophants in the room.

But Sam was silent. He's an introvert. Unlike me, who has a compulsion to process nearly all of my thoughts verbally (while everyone in the meeting has to suffer through my self-satisfying routine), Sam processes internally, not subjecting anyone to his thoughts or antics. There weren't any antics. I'm not sure there was even a pulse.

So, the meeting ends, everyone jumps into taxis to the airport and, I suspect, fiercely debates their own positions: "Do we jump on board? Do we wait this out until he forgets? Do we play along until he's bored or the strategy changes again?" I'm wise to you, people. Don't forget, I report to a leader also!

A few days pass and my phone rings with a call from Sam. Not otherwise unusual, and after a few pleasantries, he begins to deconstruct not just the meeting but literally the exact words I had used, but had completely forgotten about. Sam had precise questions about points I'd made and insightful opinions on how they would or wouldn't work going forward. His recall of the meeting was savant-like. Embarrassingly, I didn't recall saying much of what he was repeating to me, regardless of whether he agreed or disagreed. It was during and after this call that I began to better understand that the Sams of the world, just like the Scotts of the world, may operate very differently, but their value shouldn't be questioned just because their personalities differ.

Sam's precise recall of the meeting was in hindsight, the biggest compliment he could have paid me—regardless of whether that was his intention. He was clearly engrossed in the conversation (diatribe) but just chose to let others ask questions, challenge me, or become kiss-ups in the moment to garner my favor. Yes, I ran the division much like the court of Louis XVI's Versailles . . . and we know how that ended, don't we!

As an introvert—at least compared to me—Sam's communication style and ultimate influence gave me great pause as I moved on to lead other teams with differing styles. I've also adopted these insights into my parenting of three young sons, who on the surface tend to have my loud, domineering personality; but I wonder how much of that is their survival tactic in our home, and if they might be different when they're not around each other . . . and me?

Duh, I know, but how often do you find yourself in a meeting, on a phone call, watching a video conference, or any interpersonal setting where another person's style is so different from your own that you not only check out, but you begin to make sweeping, dogmatic judgments about them? "I will never work with this is person again. Do not invite me to dinner if they're coming. Their style drives me nuts." If our own self-awareness were higher, we might realize our style bothers others also. *Newsflash!*

It's not my intention to categorize introverts and extroverts finitely. I am a self-proclaimed extrovert, but I actually loathe small talk at cocktail parties and bars. I'd rather eat cauliflower than stand in a loud bar with a band and pretend I'm enjoying it. Many extroverts thrive in this environment, and I'm certain some introverts actually enjoy social interactions and then once they're done, they're done, and they're quietly gone. Unlike me, when I'm out, everyone knows it and I make sure of it. It's known as the big exit, and I'm a master at it (or so I think).

As Susan Cain helped me become aware that introverts have a unique capacity to solve difficult and complicated problems, my challenge as a leader was to create an environment where that strength could surface in real time and not have to wait for a phone call three days later.

. . .

THE TRANSFORMATIONAL INSIGHT

People like people like themselves. And leaders can fall into the same trap. So be mindful not to dismiss or minimize those around you with personalities, communication styles, and proclivities that may differ from yours.

THE QUESTION

How can you recognize when your style—be it introvert or extrovert—might be lifting or limiting the potential contribution of others?

RYAN HOLIDAY

FRANKLINCOVEY

ONLEADERSHIP

WITH SCOTT MILLER

EPISODE 87

RYAN HOLIDAY
SELF-DISCIPLINE

For those of you who know me personally or have spent hundreds of hours with me during FranklinCovey's *On Leadership* podcast, you know absolutely nothing about me reflects stillness. I haven't been still for over three minutes in my entire life. So much so, that when I opened my interview with Ryan Holiday, author of many bestselling books including *Stillness Is the Key,* I had to tell him that if I had authored the book, I would have titled it *Stillness Is Absent*. Perhaps this is why I found his writings so captivating and included him in this first volume of *Master Mentors*. Selecting from the first 150 interviews and narrowing them to 30 was no minor challenge.

Ryan is a writer and media strategist steeped in topics such as stoicism, practical philosophy, and strategic thinking. The most striking of the many transformational insights I took from Ryan's book and interview was his commitment to self-discipline—not just understanding the value of it in his life, but his *unrelenting* commitment to maintaining it. Of the many adages Dr. Stephen R. Covey was known for, "Common knowledge isn't common practice," and "To know, but not to do, is not to know," stand out here. I'm guessing those sentiments aren't original to Dr. Covey, but I will never forget them. I fully understand the value of self-discipline, but already in writing these first two paragraphs, I've checked my email, looked at and responded to multiple social posts, and told my three sons—twice now—that they can't turn on video games. Self-discipline. I get it—sort of.

My focus and self-discipline, like many people's, is situational. I loathe sitting in a multihour meeting more than I hate kale, but I can read two books on a twelve-hour flight home from Beijing almost without interruption. We often apply discipline to the areas of our life where it is easiest or provides the fastest, most immediate, and noticeable return. Ryan is a master at this in every situation, and has set firm boundaries in his life to protect him from others—and when I say others, I also mean himself. That's a transformational insight on its own: often we need to protect and save ourselves *from* ourselves.

So, what does self-discipline look like for Ryan? For one, he doesn't answer or even check his mobile phone for the first hour he's awake in the morning. He doesn't want to be jerked around by others. He instead focuses on those things that set his day deliberately on a path he creates. This means that for the first hour, he is *still*—not on the floor in monk mode, but focused, creative, and deliberate. He swims, journals, and sets his priorities based on what he wants to accomplish, not what others want or need from him.

Now, I get it; not all of us have this luxury. Especially those of us working in multinational companies where the Dubai office has been waiting patiently for you to wake your lazy ass up and answer their urgent request. But Ryan shows how we can be more deliberate in our self-discipline. Perhaps we use those excuses like the global economy and the 24/7 workday to continue living our lives like a ball pinging around in a pinball machine where the flippers and bumpers represent the various colleagues, leaders, family, and friends controlling our trajectory and sending us bouncing from one urgency to another. Great for the needs of the flippers and bumpers, but not so much for the ball. How many of us are living our lives bounced around by the needs of everyone *but* ourselves? Most of us, I suspect. Certainly me, more than I'd like.

Ryan's insights had a profound effect on me. As it happens, much of my professional success has come from my voracious reading. I read three daily newspapers (yes, in print) and so many magazine subscriptions you might think I'm a hoarder (I'm not). The hours I've logged listening to NPR in the car, NBC in the morning, and CNN in the evening are embarrassing. I'm the opposite of "ignorance is bliss," as I've taken the responsibility gene way too far in my duty as a citizen to know about every election, every foreign military coup, and every IPO or corporate merger. And my secret guilty pleasure is TMZ. How could you possibly miss whom Alec Baldwin cursed out or punched before you went to bed?

But that changed for me after my interview with Ryan. I realized I was on information overload. On top of my reading and listening habits, the podcasts, blog posts, and LinkedIn articles I'd also been consuming had grown overwhelming. I was suffocating under the weight of too much seemingly vital information. So I dialed it back. On my morning commute to the office, I turned everything off and enjoyed twenty-five minutes each way in silence—no *Morning Edition* on the way in or *All Things Considered* on the drive home. And no phone calls either, just silence. Instead, I used that time to think about the day ahead or the evening in front of me. I'd ask myself probing questions: What did I want to accomplish? What did I need to resist? Whom did I need to avoid? The self-discipline around building moments of silence allowed me to draw on the deep reservoirs of my knowledge and experience and fuel my creativity. In retrospect, I realized all my media consumption had been building a library of information in my head, but it had left me with no time to delve into it or act upon it. Same goes for the shower. It's now a media-free zone I keep sacrosanct so I can do some of my most creative thinking during the eight to ten minutes of uninterrupted time. Now, thanks to Ryan, I've added the equivalent of two or more showers to my day with zero impact on the environment.

Ryan's dedication to self-discipline reminded me of something FranklinCovey's CEO, Bob Whitman, told me. At first blush, this may sound elementary, but I've learned most profound things often do. He said, "Thinking is a legitimate business activity." I've come to appreciate this in my professional life. At the time of this writing, we're very much as a society not working in office settings. But when we were, it was odd, even unthinkable in some corporate cultures, to walk by someone's office or cubicle and see them with their feet on their desk apparently doing nothing. What a career cul-de-sac to catch someone like that. But perhaps something else was going on. Maybe this was an especially wise person who recognized the value of silence, focus, and stillness even, to collect and congeal their thoughts around a particular problem or strategy for the organization. It seems a rarity these days, as we live in a world where activity is too often mistaken for productivity. So consider turning off your Beats or AirPods and use them as silence enablers and contemplation protectors. Noise cancellation can be a beautiful thing.

Ryan Holiday's practice of self-discipline has manifested in him becoming one of the most accomplished writers of our time.

His books have sold millions of copies, and include *The Obstacle Is the Way*, *Ego Is the Enemy*, *The Daily Stoic*, and, most recently, *Lives of the Stoics: The Art of Living from Zeno to Marcus Aurelius*.

While his early books were successful, he hadn't earned a bestselling spot on the coveted *New York Times* list. But *Stillness Is the Key* launched to massive sales. A week later, when the data reports came in (most books launch on Tuesdays and sales through the following Saturday at midnight typically count toward initial bestselling status), Ryan's phone woke him up. He was in the middle of a book tour and lamentably was using his phone as an alarm clock, so he was forced to pick it up. In doing so, he noticed a flurry of texts from both his agent and publisher. Knowing it was bestseller reporting day, he summoned an inhuman amount of self-discipline and resisted checking his messages. What did he do instead? Well, you should know by now. Ryan marshaled extraordinary discipline to focus on the things that would set his day deliberately on the path he created. Only then, after his stillness hour was finished, did he look at his phone and learn *Stillness Is the Key* had earned the top spot on the *New York Times* bestseller list.

Ryan's virtue as a Master Mentor comes from invoking the self-discipline to make commitments to himself and not violate them. Now, I bet he occasionally does (we mere mortals can at least hope so as to not feel completely worthless). Either way, there are tremendous benefits in utilizing self-discipline to protect us from others and, perhaps most importantly, from ourselves. At least *most* of the time. I plan on checking every email, text, and website the day this book is eligible for any bestseller list.

. . .

THE TRANSFORMATIONAL INSIGHT

We often think of self-discipline as being focused on doing something in particular. And although that certainly is true, exercising the self-discipline *not* to do something can exponentiate your creativity and productivity.

THE QUESTION

If you were to establish a greater degree of self-discipline tomorrow, is there one recurring habit that, if you could improve upon, modify, or even eliminate, would have a disproportionately positive impact on both your confidence and your ability to progress something enormously important to you?

NELY GALÁN

FRANKLINCOVEY
ONLEADERSHIP
WITH SCOTT MILLER

EPISODE 29

NELY GALÁN
HYPE YOUR FAILURES

Nely Galán is my sister from another mother. First, we both relentlessly pursue our goals and are unabashedly willing to share our failures along the way. Second, we both realize and teach that there is great value in having a relationship with fear and failure. To quote Nely, "Not only is it a relationship, but fear and failure must become your best friend."

Nely is a force of nature. Her list of accomplishments is too long to spell out (and she would tell you so is her list of failures). She's the author of *Self Made*, is the nation's first Latina president of a US television network (Telemundo), the producer of over six hundred television episodes in both English and Spanish, and went on a wild run on *Celebrity Apprentice* with Donald Trump, where she raised $250,000 for the charity Count Me In. Her energy is absolutely contagious. Recently she's transformed her brand into a real estate developer and she's coaching thousands of female entrepreneurs and those with simple side hustles to "Buy buildings, not shoes!" Nely is in constant motion and recently earned a PhD in clinical psychology. I could keep going, but there's more to learn from her failures than her successes.

Nely immigrated to the United States from Cuba as a young girl, and worked tirelessly to build her skills and influence—and a burgeoning media empire. Like many celebrities and business moguls, you meet them after their tipping point. Most of us were introduced to her on *Celebrity Apprentice* without knowing the path she blazed to get there. We only see the train pulling into the station, whistles blowing, steam billowing, and every cabin gleaming. Hidden from view is the ironworks twelve states away with workers covered in soot forging spikes and track, or laborers clearing trees and brush and flattening land to lay hundreds of miles of track. We're spared the sight of engines going off the tracks and taking dozens of cars with them, or bridges collapsing under too much weight and the countless collisions that came with the developing handcar industry. Got the visual?

We just board the train at the station and enjoy the ride. We rarely see the track being laid far in front of us.

Nely laid track for decades. And much of it she will tell you was bent and unusable. But trains don't travel in straight lines, and even bent track can be put to use. Okay, enough about trains. The transformational insight here is: don't be fooled into thinking there is anything such as an overnight success; and on that long journey, don't hide your failures but rather hype them, embrace them, and openly share them with others as a coach and mentor.

There is a connection between hard work and hyping failures—whether failures come as the inevitable by-product of effort, or failures serve as the springboard to stand up, dust yourself off, and get back to work. Consider the careers of people like Justin Bieber, Venus and Serena Williams, Gwen Stefani, Martha Stewart, Tim Tebow, Rachel Hollis, Taylor Swift, Ellen DeGeneres, Diane von

Furstenberg, Jennifer Lopez, Harrison Ford . . . just to name a few. Some began early in life and discovered fame and success quickly. For most others (nearly all), it was decades of honing their craft to build their skills, brand, and reputation. Does anyone think the Williams sisters burst on the tennis scene because of connections and a skilled agent? Do we believe Harrison Ford grew up with the casting director of *Star Wars* and just landed the spot? Hardly. Look at Ford's career prior to *Star Wars*, and you will have an entirely new appreciation for his journey.

Consider Rachel Hollis. Do we think Rachel, who sold nearly five million books last year, simply woke up one day and found herself on *Good Morning America*? Nope. That feat took more than fifteen years of hard work and many personal and professional failures along the way—you never fully arrive at success without failing somewhere daily. Rachel toiled as a food-and-lifestyle blogger and an event planner for a decade-plus. She wrote and published six other books few even know about. Then number seven, *Girl, Wash Your Face*, followed by *Girl, Stop Apologizing* exploded onto the scene. Then she founded a company, and within two years was hosting stadium-size events with tens of thousands of people paying several hundred dollars to listen to her life and business wisdom. The event is three days of her sharing some of what she's done right but more of what she's done wrong and how to learn and grow from it. If you've seen Rachel at one of these events, you've been in awe of her influence. Together, her two most recent books sold more than any other author in 2019 except former First Lady Michelle Obama. Ever heard of *Smart Girl*, *Sweet Girl*, or *Party Girl*? No? EXACTLY! Those were three of her first books. Rachel Hollis wrote six books before the world noticed her—at least in any significant capacity.

Her track laying is exactly what Nely is speaking to—show the struggle to teach success. To quote Nely, "We all promote what we do and hype up our successes. But in fact, we should be hyping up our failures . . . to have two or three major successes in my life, I've got to have thousands of failures."[1] Kudos to Nely, and to Rachel, for owning their failures and learning from them.

Nely Galán didn't become the country's first Latina television-network president merely because she spoke Spanish. She laid track for decades—working in every industry role, learning the ropes at every level. Her lesson is simple: there are no shortcuts in life—certainly not in business. Most people know Elon Musk for what? Tesla, of course. Few have any idea about his role at eBay. In fact, Elon had at least five significant business ventures before he joined Tesla. I don't know him personally (maybe I'll invite him on the podcast), but I bet not every venture ended up like Tesla and there were some hard-won lessons learned along the way.

So put in the work. Document your misses and your setbacks—don't simply learn from them but teach from them. The best leaders are those like Nely Galán who not only own their messes but highlight them, showcase them, and make it safe for others to own theirs as well. Too few leaders are comfortable showing the railroad tie that gave way, or the calloused hands that hammered it in. Too often we only see the highly polished leader free from the wear and tear of having made the long journey to reach that point. To which I call B.S.! People want to relate to their leaders and learn from their mistakes. Your colleagues want to be led by a genuine person with real failures and enough courage to talk about them.

Don't just hype your successes. Take Nely's advice and hype your failures! Then see what a difference it makes. Speaking of making a difference, it was after reading Nely's book, *Self Made*, and completing her *On Leadership* interview that I was inspired to write and publish my first book, *Management Mess to*

Leadership Success. I basically spent the entire manuscript highlighting my own messes so that others could learn from them. Thank you, Nely, for giving me the courage to do so and for modeling the power of hyping *your* failures.

. . .

THE TRANSFORMATIONAL INSIGHT

The most successful and influential people achieve that stature not just by experiencing failure but hyping their failures for the benefit of others.

THE QUESTION

Which failure of yours, if revisited and publicized, could transform someone else's confidence into their own successful journey?

LEIF BABIN

FRANKLINCOVEY
ONLEADERSHIP
WITH SCOTT MILLER

EPISODE 75

LEIF BABIN
EXTREME OWNERSHIP

I'd seen the books *Extreme Ownership* and *The Dichotomy of Leadership* by Jocko Willink and Leif Babin at the bookstore for several years. I knew both titles were *New York Times* bestsellers and that the authors were increasingly renowned speakers and popular podcast hosts and guests. But as I mentioned in chapter ten, featuring General McChrystal, I have almost no personal military history or connections, and thus don't gravitate to that genre of books. (Don't overanalyze that statement, as it's not an opinion or a lack of respect for the military in any form. It's the same reason I don't read books about the keto diet, horse racing, or crocheting—just not my thing.)

But the books stared at me weekly on my Saturday trips with my sons to the local bookstore, and I finally couldn't resist the lure any longer. Supporting print books in local bookstores, accompanied by my sons, is one of my favorite things to do in life. My wife shops online. I drive to bookstores—even during a pandemic with masks on and hands washed afterward.

Two days later, I finished *Extreme Ownership*—by then also a *Wall Street Journal* bestseller with over a million copies sold—and it captivated me. It's a superb read—more of a manual, really. The perfect book to buy for all of your team leaders to read a chapter a week and debrief it as a book club. Both authors are former Navy SEALs who share leadership lessons from their riveting, moment-by-moment missions in Ramadi, Iraq. Their writing style is gripping. Regardless of your opinion about the American presence in Iraq, the lessons they teach are piercingly insightful and surprisingly relevant in the business, nonprofit, and public sector. That may be a duh for you, but it wasn't for me. I thought I would need to translate every chapter from a combat situation into *my world*. I fully expected to read some great military stories, followed by me having to adapt the lessons learned and make them relevant to a CMO or executive vice president's role.

I was wrong—no translation or adaptation needed.

Leif and Jocko do a masterful job of seamlessly moving between life-and-death experiences in Iraq, and teaching you how to apply those lessons in your business. I've read thousands of business and leadership books over my career, and nobody has done this better than these two gentlemen heroes.

So, of course, I had to interview Leif for the podcast. Gracious, wise, and, as you would expect, clear and determined on his thoughts and actions, Leif attended the US Naval Academy and spoke to the impact *The 7 Habits of Highly Effective People* had on him during his time there. (It's a part of their leadership curriculum.) After graduating from the academy, Leif was not selected to become a SEAL. The program only takes fifteen out of a graduating class of nine hundred, which was a bummer for him, since becoming a SEAL was his lifelong dream.

Fast-forward several years and Leif finally got in. He then spent nine years as a Navy SEAL with three separate combat tours in Iraq, followed by becoming a leadership instructor for graduating SEAL officers. To give you some sense for the rigor of the program, Leif's SEAL class began with a 193 candidates, of which 44 graduated to become SEALs. Keep in mind that there are only about 3,500 active SEALs in service, out of around a hundred times that number serving in the active US Navy.

I would not qualify, as sharks and jellyfish keep me close to shore with the water always below my knees. (That's what happens when you're raised in Florida and are acutely aware of what's really going on in the ocean.) Let's just say I am grateful for the navy.

Now to the transformational insight. Unsurprisingly, it lies in the book title: *Extreme Ownership*. Leif told me, "It's a mindset and an attitude. And without it, you're never going to actually do what you need to do to solve problems and win. Extreme Ownership simply means there's no one else to blame. There are no excuses. You've got to own everything in your world; not just what you're responsible for. You have to own every single thing that impacts you."[1] He went on to say, "Once leaders recognize this is all on me, then [they are] going to actually have to do the hard work to get the team where they need to go—to train people, to mentor people."[2]

He calls it simple, not easy. It's not a hard concept to understand, but it's incredibly difficult to apply in real life. Because there is something in the human condition—in our psyche—that makes us want to make excuses, point fingers, and cast blame. When we do, the pressing problems we face never get solved. But when the leader sets the tone of "I own this, I am responsible, and we're going to do everything in our power to solve these problems," Leif says it builds a culture where you do actually solve problems and win. His and Jocko's research and experience shows that when leaders across every sector of industry, not just the military, lived this principle, they experienced transformative results.

Now, in case you're thinking Leif is recommending that by *owning* everything, the leader has to *do* everything, fear not. Leif differentiates between centralized command (where the leader's mindset is they must do it all themselves) versus decentralized command (where leaders must in fact solve problems at their own level). Utilizing a decentralized approach creates clarity on the mission and ensures everyone is working toward the same goal.

In our interview, Leif opens the book about a situation in the military called "blue-on-blue," or friendly fire. Read the book or listen to the podcast for the entire story, but here was the big takeaway for me: the worst military situation to be in is a blue-on-blue incident. The authors' unit found themselves in one during an intense firefight that killed an Iraqi soldier and wounded one of their SEALs. According to Leif, this is every military leader's worst nightmare, and the snowball effect that ensues often results in the leader being fired. Because of the deadly incident, the commanding officer shut down the operation and investigating officers descended on the team. During this time, Jocko, as the leader of the operation, gathered every member of the team and began the debrief. And true to what Jocko and Leif teach in the book, every team member took full responsibility for what they could have done differently in their respective roles, including radio communication, line-of-sight communication, better positive identification, and so on. Then Jocko looked at every member and announced with no equivocation that *he* was responsible. *He* owned the results of the failed operation and took complete responsibility with the commanding officer. That's why, in this rare case of a blue-on-blue incident, Jocko was, in fact, not fired. The commanding officer actually gained trust in him when he saw that serious solutions were being implemented to ensure nothing like that ever happened again. That's Extreme Ownership.

Jocko's example reminds me of a situation at FranklinCovey several years back. No comparison in terms of gravity and loss of life, but memorable nonetheless. Our company was transitioning from being an extremely successful traditional training company—where nearly all of our clients globally consumed our content and solutions in a physical classroom—to becoming a SaaS (software as a service) company, where many of our solutions were available digitally and consumed through blended learning, live and asynchronous webinars, and in many cases designed for self-paced, on-demand learning. Our CEO, Bob Whitman, was leading a massive transition of our business and offerings to ensure we would be competitive for years to come by pivoting to a licensing-and-enterprise-wide subscription model now known as Franklin-Covey's All Access Pass for our organizational clients. That's not a pitch, but a setup for what came next.

This massive overhaul of our company disrupted every system, structure, way of thinking, and collaboration among teams. It required a complete shift in how we designed products and solutions, how we marketed them to prospects, and how our field sales teams adapted their own skills and understanding of how to sell and service current and future clients. It was like flying a plane and changing the engines in midair. As a public company, we needed to maintain our revenue and profitability as we fundamentally changed everything we'd known for over thirty-five years. There were no metaphorical planes to park in hangars and convert. All of the planes needed to stay in the air during the transformation.

Fast-forward about twelve months into launch, and we'd learned a tremendous amount from our clients about the need to upgrade our portal and its user interface functionality. We needed to enhance both the administrator and user experience and how we further addressed security and data protection. These issues are common to every company transitioning their business models toward technology platforms, but that didn't make it any easier. Let's just say promises were made to the sales colleagues in the field, then they made those same promises to our valuable clients. Dates. Specific deliverables. Reputations at stake.

And then those promises and deadlines were violated.

Because of a variety of factors, internal commitments evaporated, and it became clear, even after daily hours-long accountability meetings led by our CEO, that the outside vendor contracted to make the portal upgrades would not come through. Not a long-term miss, but the dates we'd promised our sales associates for an upgraded portal experience could not be kept. It was impossible. (Believe me, the CEO tried.)

Reality sank in during one especially tense executive team meeting, and Bob, after every attempt to keep the commitments, announced the only option was to schedule a companywide call and immediately share the news. I'll spare you the play-by-play logistics, but within twenty-four hours, our CEO sat in the company boardroom, on camera with hundreds of company associates, and talked straight. He walked the team through the highlights, with no excuses or finger-pointing at those who had failed to deliver (and there were plenty of them internally and externally), and took full responsibility for the miss. He didn't obfuscate. He didn't spin or posture. He told the truth and owned it. He also didn't promise a date we would fix it. Rather, he promised full transparency and timely updates going forward.

I recall pacing around the boardroom watching the CEO, who we all greatly respected, address the issue head on and take Extreme Ownership in front of hundreds of associates who then needed to go back to their clients and break promises, and unwind and recalibrate expectations—and perhaps, even as painful, explain to their spouses and partners why their incomes might be adversely impacted because of delayed sales and commissions.

It was brutal.

Painful.

Admirable.

The portal was eventually upgraded and launched, but not in hours, days, or even weeks. It took several months, because that's what was required to deliver it with FranklinCovey quality.

No leader wants to be placed in this situation. The sales staff was not pleased. Many were understanding; many were angry. Some perhaps even temporarily disillusioned. But what they all shared was a trust that Bob had set the standard by which every leader in the company would operate: Extreme Ownership.

The insights shared from Leif Babin and his coauthor, Jocko Willink, make *Extreme Ownership* a must-read for any leader at any level. When leaders transform their mindset to Extreme Ownership, it models that same transformative behavior that not only is successful on the battlefield but in every organization, team, and even your family.

. . .

THE TRANSFORMATIONAL INSIGHT

When your team members see you own not just the successes, but the outright failures with no finger-pointing, you set the only acceptable standard.

THE QUESTION

Ask yourself: *Do I demonstrate Extreme Ownership across every area of my life—professionally and personally?*

STEDMAN GRAHAM

FRANKLINCOVEY
ONLEADERSHIP
WITH SCOTT MILLER

EPISODE 107

STEDMAN GRAHAM
CHOOSE YOUR IDENTITY

Ever thought much about your identity? I'll admit, I hadn't really given the topic much thought until I read Stedman Graham's advice that, "You can also think of identity as your personal brand."[1]

Bam!

Now that's something I *have* been thinking about for a very long time. In fact, I wrote an entire book on corporate and personal brands called *Marketing Mess to Brand Success: 30 Challenges to Transform Your Organization's Brand (And Your Own)*. But I'm going to take a slightly different insight from Stedman's work on identity. His most recent book is called *Identity Leadership: To Lead Others You Must First Lead Yourself*.

After spending my entire career in the personal-development industry, I'd invested a significant amount of effort in understanding mindsets, belief windows, paradigms, motivations, goals, and our behaviors as drivers of our successes, setbacks, and failures.

I've also come to believe that we frequently form our identities from what others think about us. Unlike our reputations, we can't completely control the narratives formed by other people. A great deal of how others perceive us is the result of happenstance—from bad timing, bad luck, or misfortune. Such is life. But that doesn't negate the intentionality we should build and own around our reputation, which is simply the sum total of the decisions we've made in life.

Unless you're an elected official and have a voting record (which I'm currently not), it's impossible for people who only know you casually or socially to see the full picture of who you are. I've lived in five major metropolitan cities spread across nineteen different homes and neighborhoods. In each, I've had different friends and neighbors, and none of the people I've rented from, bought from, sold to, lived next to, or befriended have had a complete experience with me. Really, besides my parents and my wife, most people who have an opinion about me construct it based on a handful of experiences, some of which might be unbelievably positive and others nightmarishly negative.

I have supporters and I have detractors, and I likely deserve both; but my point is, we're judged in short bursts, in a variety of settings, through narrow points of view, and rarely when we're at our best. Often in a professional setting, many form an opinion or come to a conclusion about me after a meeting or two or after standing together in a trade-show booth for a few hours. No one's reputation—or, for that matter, identity—should be tied to distinct moments in time.

Our identities are far more complex, nuanced, and Gordian.

Here's what I mean: I'm a rather intense person, and people tell me this all the time. It's never said to me as a compliment; more of a jab of sorts, which over time I've moved from finding annoying to amusing. I've also been told that I never slow down, can't relax, and it must be really hard for me to take a vacation.

To the extent I care about shaping that narrative in others, my wife, Stephanie, will sometimes (not enough) step in and gently correct them. Join me in Greece or Italy for a week, and we're lying by the pool pretty much the entire time—reading, drinking, laughing, and ordering food. It's common that I arrive, plant myself by the pool until it's time to shower and dress for dinner (possibly poolside), and decompress from my self-imposed sustained and annoying intensity. I also love the go-go-go vacation where tours are booked, souvenirs collected, and itineraries followed. Depending on which vacation you joined me for, your view of my chillness could be wildly divergent. Extrapolate on that one vacation experience to form a wider opinion of who I am, and I end up being both the person who never leaves the pool and the person who never slows down enough to even find a pool. So which one is true?

Both.

Neither.

And that's the problem.

When our identity is prescribed by those who have just a small frame of reference, they will inevitably get it wrong. Which means, outside of your spouse, significant other, close family members, or a close friend and confidante, nobody—let's repeat, *nobody*—is going to get it right. Not even your accountant (but they might get close).

Stedman instilled in me the concept that we invest too much time and attention in *finding* our identities and managing what others think about us based on a few encounters. Nor should we be continually chasing the goals others want for us when they declare how we should spend our time, money, or energy. How many of us followed an educational or professional path our parents hammered into us instead of doing what we wanted for ourselves? How many of us felt obligated to follow our parents' lead because we were conditioned (by them) that they were next to infallible and knew what was best? How many of us followed our parents' career prescriptions out of a sense of guilt, since they were the ones who sacrificed to fund our schooling in the first place? And how many of us did all this without even entertaining the thought our parents could be redeeming their own sense of failure and shortcomings through their children's future accomplishments? That may require late-night carb-bingeing and a few visits to the therapist to get through and unpack, but I'm sure it's the case for many. Probably far too many.

What if we stopped trying to *find* our identities altogether and instead *created* them ourselves? As Stedman writes: "Building your identity is about knowing what your calling is, learning how to do it well, and creating value in the world. I've learned that, for the most part, extraordinary people are simply ordinary people doing extraordinary things that matter to them."[2]

That matter to *them* (meaning you). That's the key.

Not what matters to well-intentioned (and especially ill-intentioned) associates, friends, neighbors, clergy, parents, educators, counselors, or the myriad authors who will sell you books and have an opinion about who, what, and how you should think about your identity (including me). Stop looking for the answers from the outside. Rather, intentionally create your own identity for yourself.

This insight and choice of identity lays the path toward identity leadership, which Stedman calls a form of self-leadership. He suggests that identity leadership comprises four facets: self-awareness, self-management, other-awareness, and other-management. Stedman lays these aspects out in a purposefully linear order: "You have to be self-aware before you can learn how to be a self-manager and nurture your abilities, emotions, and leadership capacities. And you need both self-awareness and self-management before you can be aware of others' needs and potential. And you need that other-awareness before you can grow the potential in others."[3]

On the day I finalized this chapter, actor Elliot Page (star of the films *Juno* and *Inception*) came out as transgender. Now, I rarely look at Hollywood stars as role models for my life, but I can't help but appreciate the timeliness of his building and declaring his identity as I'm putting the last touches on a chapter of the same name. "I can't begin to express how remarkable it feels to finally love who I am enough to pursue my authentic self," Page wrote on his social media. "The more I hold myself close and fully embrace who I am, the more I dream, the more my heart grows and the more I thrive."

I'm certain Stedman Graham, like the vast majority of us, would agree.

. . .

THE TRANSFORMATIONAL INSIGHT

Cease fulfilling the identity foisted upon you by others and, instead, create the identity that best leverages your passions, talents, and dreams. Be the version of yourself you want to be.

THE QUESTION

How will you create the identity that helps you pursue your "extraordinary" thing?

LIZ WISEMAN

FRANKLINCOVEY
ONLEADERSHIP
WITH SCOTT MILLER

EPISODE 4

LIZ WISEMAN

BE A MULTIPLIER AND NOT A DIMINISHER

I KNOW A powerful book when I read one and enjoy pollinating them across my network. This one is *Multipliers: How the Best Leaders Make Everyone Smarter* by Liz Wiseman. I have thoroughly enjoyed every book highlighted in this tome, but I am very comfortable stating that *Multipliers* is my favorite leadership book ever written. A close second is *Radical Candor* by Kim Scott (chapter eleven). Fortunately, Liz and Kim are friends and both know how instrumental their books have been in my own leadership journey.

Liz is one of the world's foremost leadership authorities and is arguably one of the most in-demand speakers globally on the topic. I'd wager she's the most frequently featured female speaker in the leadership space. We all read books that are hit-or-miss for us, often based on the timing of when we read them. Perhaps a book might haunt or inspire us because we're facing the exact issue it addresses while we're reading it. Other books might feel less valuable for the same reason but hit someone else in their own sweet spot. The former describes my experience with Liz and *Multipliers*. You'd think that after thirty years in the leadership industry and twenty-five with FranklinCovey, I'd rate one of our books as my favorite. That feels too convenient to me. Yes, our firm has sold over fifty million copies of our books and I have been part of writing, editing, and launching many of them. But *Multipliers* remains my favorite. Here's why, and it's the basis for this chapter.

Liz spent nearly all of her professional career with Oracle. As an early employee of the firm, she rose quickly and became the vice president of Oracle University and global leader for human resource development. Post-Oracle, she founded The Wiseman Group, and invested nearly a decade researching and writing what became several bestselling books. At heart, Liz will tell you she's an observer and a researcher. She enjoys watching people work and lead, for good and for bad, and that's what inspired *Multipliers*. The book proposes that, daily, each of us is both multiplying and accidentally diminishing people. We're not one or the other—a Multiplier or a Diminisher—but rather we're constantly doing both. With increased awareness, we can multiply more and diminish less.

Sounds easy. But then, most leadership concepts do, even though we all know they often aren't.

Buy the book to learn more about the nine Accidental Diminisher tendencies. I don't want this chapter to be a book review, but let's just say I sadly identified with them all. I'll throw you a bone with the list of nine and then speak to the one that changed me entirely. They are: *Idea Fountain* (updated from *Idea Guy* in an early version of the book), *Always On*, *Rescuer*, *Pacesetter*, *Rapid Responder*, *Optimist*, *Protector*, *Strategist*, and *Perfectionist*.

Beyond this list of Accidental Diminisher tendencies, the premise of the book is that nobody wants to work for the smartest person in the room. As leaders, our role is not to be the genius, but rather the genius maker of others. When I read the book and first interviewed Liz, I was horrified. It felt like someone had pulled the covers back and there I was, naked and not exactly sporting a six-pack (sorry for the visual folks).

I learned an immense amount about my leadership style from Liz's research and insights. It's comforting to know I'm not alone, which is why it became a *New York Times* bestseller. I honestly never really made it past the first Accidental Diminisher tendency—the Idea Fountain. I became almost transfixed with how accurate it was in summing up my role as FranklinCovey's chief marketing officer. My influence, power, longevity, value, and survivability all came from being the company's Idea Fountain. I was so adept at branding (some might say anointing) myself the Idea Fountain that the CEO, who does not suffer fools lightly, invited me into meetings far beyond my areas of responsibility (and likely, even competence). He came to see me as such. (Hey, I was pretty good at marketing after all . . .)

I've written extensively and vulnerably in my *Mess to Success* series about why I felt the need to be the Idea Fountain (short answer: mainly my insecurities). But what I'd like to share here is the impact it had not only on other members of the marketing team, but also how it affected the overall company strategy—not always positively.

I built and earned a solid reputation for delivering results in my role as CMO, as evidenced by the continued support of the CEO, CFO, board of directors, and other members of the executive team. But what I also built (perhaps less obvious to them at the time) was a continued contribution of distraction. As the team's Idea Fountain, I was a walking buffet of options. Morrison's and Piccadilly had nothing on me. I came to believe that my chief value was the phrase "What if we were to . . . ?" As I reflect on this, I shudder to think how many thousands of times I offered that up—often unsolicited, followed by a metaphorical cornucopia of ideas, solutions, and, ultimately, distractions.

Why distractions? Isn't a marketer's job to offer solutions? What else are you supposed to do—just be quiet and listen?

Well, yes, sometimes. And I sucked at it. I was often the veritable solution searching for a problem. All this confessing is to share with you that my razzmatazz could be so successful—even with immensely qualified leaders—that, because of my influence, I could be very distracting. It wasn't always noticeable in the moment; but as I look back, I was often responsible for "winning the battle" at the expense of "losing the war." Perhaps that's an exaggeration, but too many of my ideas became diminishing as they risked turning into a steady stream of distractions with the current tidal wave sometimes pulling away from the firm's overall strategy. What I thought were ideas that could save the day were, in fact, just that—ideas that would save the *day*. But the day didn't always need saving if we could build the capacity and discipline to ensure that, companywide, we learned to avoid or overcome the risk altogether. I had become both the Idea Fountain *and* the genius in the room—a combination that could easily succumb to a number of risks, both strategic and interpersonal.

Since my time with Liz and two *On Leadership* interviews with her, I stepped away from the CMO role of my own volition, as I felt it was the best strategy for my growth while allowing others in the marketing division to nurture their own ideas and creativity. Truly, stepping aside at the right time was—and I say this with some humility in mind—a gift to the organization. My contribution in that specific role needed to end.

Now I don't mean to suggest that quitting a job or stepping away is the answer to becoming a Multiplier. Hardly. Seven years in the position was plenty, and there were other opportunities in the firm I needed and wanted to lead. I love to disrupt myself; it's likely the key to why I got to step away on my own terms instead of being asked to step away on someone else's.

We should all think deeply about what triggers us to be Diminishers in our interactions with others. In my case, I often lacked the discretion for when to "fountain" in a way that was helpful versus distracting, although I'm confident that when the CEO reads this chapter, he will be more charitable on my tenure as CMO than I've described here. But that really isn't important; self-awareness is. It's vital for leaders to know their strengths and weaknesses—when you're multiplying and when you're diminishing. And then it's important to show the humility and vulnerability to confront and openly talk about them. Not only in your head, but with others you trust to help you develop a strategy to become a better leader and Multiplier.

Read Liz's book and identify which of the nine Accidental Diminishers tendencies you relate to. Then ask some colleagues for their independent assessment. There's no shame in owning your diminishing tendencies; the shame is in willfully ignoring them.

. . .

THE TRANSFORMATIONAL INSIGHT

Multiplying leaders possess not only the self-awareness to recognize when they could be accidentally diminishing others but create and allow space for others to feel smart around them.

THE QUESTION

Do you tend to be the genius in the room or the genius maker of others? How can you become more multiplying and less diminishing in your interactions?

JAY PAPASAN

FRANKLINCOVEY
ONLEADERSHIP
WITH SCOTT MILLER

EPISODE 66

JAY PAPASAN
THE ONE THING

In 2008, Jay Papasan was leading Keller Williams's in-house university and was designing a new course for their associates. In case the name Keller Williams isn't readily recognizable to you, it is the United States' largest residential real estate company with 170,000 agents worldwide. Not too shabby. Gary Keller, the co-founder, took Jay's new course home to rework the opening in preparation for it going live. The course was targeted at agents with the goal of increasing their own small real estate businesses enough to afford their executive assistants, and what better way to inspire them than an opening from the brand's namesake.

Gary came back with a new, eight-page introduction titled "The Power of One," and Jay responded with, "Gary, this feels like a book." That was the genesis of the bestselling *The ONE Thing: The Surprisingly Simple Truth Behind Extraordinary Results* by Gary Keller with Jay Papasan. The book covered the shelves of every airport bookstore in the United States for years. First published in 2013, the book's premise rests on a simple truth from Gary Keller's life and career as a self-made billionaire: "Where I'd had huge success, I had narrowed my concentration to one thing, and where my success varied, my focus had too."[1]

Yep, another book recommendation from Scott Miller. I love print books, by the way. When I buy them at my local bookstore, the first thing I do when I arrive home is take off the cover and place it somewhere safe on my desk so I don't rip or tear it while reading. Then, once consumed, the cover goes back on and the book heads to the bookcase in our living room, where inevitably during a dinner party, I will jump up, retrieve it, tell someone they absolutely must read it, then impulsively give it to them (which is why I buy two copies of most books). Excessive? Yes. Wise? Debatable. Fun? Oh, hell yes!

Regarding *The ONE Thing,* I found this book so valuable that one evening, to the horror of every school librarian around the world, I tore out page 150.

Shriek! How many Hail Marys and Our Fathers will I need to say for that one?

This book is *pure gold, people.* But why page 150? Buy it, and you'll see. Here's a hint: Gary and Jay repeat throughout the book, countless times, a single question that becomes a mantra: "What's the ONE Thing I can do such that by doing it, everything else would be easier or unnecessary?"

Huh? I'm going to repeat it more slowly for you (this is where you now read this line v-e-r-y s-l-o-w-l-y). What's the ONE Thing I can do such that by doing it, everything else will be easier or unnecessary?

It's so simple, it's profound. Jay further offers in the book that, as easy as the question is to get your head around, "The ONE Thing becomes difficult, because we've unfortunately bought in to too many others—and more often than not, those 'other things' muddle our thinking, misguide our actions, and sidetrack our success."[2]

Hasn't he just described your life? He has mine. I'm going to digress for just a moment. To be invited to appear as a guest on FranklinCovey's *On Leadership with Scott Miller* podcast, you need to jump a few hurdles. None of the guests knew this (until now), but the questions look like this:

- Do they have something unique and valuable to offer our subscribers, listeners, and viewers (although it's technically a podcast, about 50 percent of folks consume it visually) around the topic of leadership?
- If they've authored a book, how will the content immediately improve the skills of our listeners and viewers?
- Is the guest reputable? Trustworthy? Do they align with our own brand and reputation?
- Will their point of view and field of experience challenge our listeners and viewers to think differently?
- With only fifty-two episodes annually, does their gravitas warrant taking a spot for our global audience to invest their time in?
- And perhaps most importantly, does Scott respect them? (Not really a requirement, but it sure helps.) Seriously, though, are they engaging, easy to schedule, and do they care about our audience? You can feel, hear, and see it if the answer is no.
- Jay hit every category. A+.

The reason I ripped out page 150 is because it illustrates a transformative goal-setting process I think everyone can relate to and execute, whether you're a billionaire founder of a company looking to expand your global footprint, or a stay-at-home parent saving for a new dishwasher, or a small entrepreneur looking for your first (or second) paying client. Again, so simple, it's profound. With their permission, I've recapped the wisdom from page 150 for "Goal Setting to the Now":

- Someday Goal: What's the ONE Thing I want to do someday?

- Five-Year Goal: Based on my Someday Goal, what's the ONE Thing I can do in the next five years?

- One-Year Goal: Based on my Five-Year Goal, what's the ONE Thing I can do this year?

- Monthly Goal: Based on my One-Year Goal, what's the ONE Thing I can do this month?

- Weekly Goal: Based on my Monthly Goal, what's the ONE Thing I can do this week?

- Daily Goal: Based on my Weekly Goal, what's the ONE Thing I can do today?

- Right Now: Based on my Daily Goal, what's the ONE Thing I can do right now?

I wonder how few of us have ever articulated our Someday Goal. That's the first step in their process of Goal Setting to the Now. I could write more words to meet my editor's quota here, but I won't. Instead, take the six hundred words I would have added below and answer these seven questions for yourself. And make sure you do it; otherwise, I'll have to answer to my editor at HarperCollins Leadership about my lackadaisical writing habits. Ready? Here we go:

- Someday Goal: What's the ONE Thing you want to do someday? ____________________

  ____

  ____

  ____

- Five-Year Goal: Based on your Someday Goal, what's the ONE Thing you can do in the next five years? ____________________

  ____

  ____

  ____

- One-Year Goal: Based on your Five-Year Goal, what's the ONE Thing you can do this year? ____________________

  ____

  ____

  ____

- Monthly Goal: Based on your One-Year Goal, what's the ONE Thing you can do this month? ____________________

  ____

  ____

  ____

- Weekly Goal: Based on your Monthly Goal, what's the ONE Thing you can do this week? ____________________

  ____

  ____

  ____

- Daily Goal: Based on your Weekly Goal, what's the ONE Thing you can do today? ______________________________
____
____
____

- Right Now: Based on your Daily Goal, what's the ONE Thing you can do right now? __________________________
____
____
____

For those of us easily distracted from our own goals, don't feel empowered to achieve them, or work for a leader who doesn't care about them, try this response from Jay on for size: "A request must be connected to my ONE Thing for me to consider it."

Bold but certainly transformational!

. . .

THE TRANSFORMATIONAL INSIGHT

Achieving any level of goal necessitates that you follow both a systematic and pragmatic approach that, ultimately, results in you doing something different . . . right now.

THE QUESTION

Did you skip the exercise above? If you did, not only are you a horrible goal setter, but you're never going accomplish your Someday Goal . . . because you don't even know what it is. Do not pass GO. Do not collect $200. Go back and do the exercise.

SETH GODIN

FRANKLINCOVEY
ONLEADERSHIP
WITH SCOTT MILLER

EPISODE 12

SETH GODIN
FEARLESS VS. RECKLESS

I FIRST LEARNED about Seth Godin when I read his book *Purple Cow*. It's since become a classic along with many others including *Tribes*, *Linchpin*, and his most recent titles, *This Is Marketing* and *The Practice*. After subscribing to his daily blog (he hasn't missed a day in over twelve years), I reached out to him a decade ago regarding some collaborations with FranklinCovey. True to his brand and writings, his generosity and magnanimity were on display when he invited me to his office outside New York City where I was joined by our Chief People Officer, Todd Davis (featured in chapter twenty-two).

Todd and I arrived for what we thought would be a short meeting when Seth met us at the door, ushered us in, and immediately made us lunch. And when I say, "made us lunch," I don't mean he opened a platter of catered sandwiches, which in and of itself would have been a pleasant surprise, but this gentleman had gone to the trouble to shop for fresh ingredients and then sautéed veggies and made a delicious stir-fry. All while learning about our personal interests and passions as well as our families and backgrounds. This all happened long before we talked about anything business-related, and set in motion a ten-year friendship where I've become, as Ken Blanchard would say, a raving fan.

Seth was naturally one of the first guests I invited to appear on the *On Leadership* podcast, and he also graciously endorsed my first book, *Management Mess to Leadership Success*. In the intervening years, I've likely learned more from Seth than anyone else in my adult life. Above all would be the concept of being fearless as opposed to reckless. I think many of us often confuse the two.

At first blush, like perhaps many of the transformational insights I share here, this may seem like a no-brainer. *Got it. Don't confuse fearless behavior with reckless behavior*. But as Voltaire wrote, "Common sense is not so common." If it were, I'd be eating a lot more kale, broccoli, and spinach and a lot less bread, butter, and cheese.

It's easy to embrace fearlessness as a strength: the pre-permission for boldness, bravado, speaking up/out/against/with, and telling the hard truths. And there's something to that. Speaking one's mind requires a good deal of courage in the face of losing friends, breaking up the dinner party, or even damaging a relationship. At work, such recklessness disguised as fearlessness can damage reputations, demotivate teams, poison a thriving culture, and put the brakes on productivity—all because being "fearless" can be intoxicating and even addicting. It's a convenient label we hang on a host of behaviors, consequences be damned. Being fearless, like many strengths, can be overdone and turn into something else. Too often what we call being fearless is actually being reckless.

So, what's the difference?

I'd spent most of my adult life convinced I was acting fearlessly. In my twenties, I moved across the country from Florida to Utah, where I spoke and acted in ways that left no doubt I wasn't a part of the dominant culture. I relished being the "I can't believe he went there" guy at work as well, and made an outspoken and unfiltered communication style part of my brand. I wore my sense of fearlessness like a badge of honor. But one of the key differences between acting fearlessly and acting recklessly is acknowledging who it is you're *really* serving.

Being reckless feeds the ego, is detached from character, and is more impulsive than thoughtful and more myopic than prescient. In short, one hallmark of being reckless is *selfishness,* and one trait of being fearless is *selflessness*. Again, the question to ask is, "Who am I serving by doing this?"

Meeting with Seth, I came to realize that, in much of my life, I'd confused being fearless with being reckless, and spent too many years thinking and then saying the same thing. I had zero verbal filter. If it came into my mind, it came out of my mouth. I convinced myself this was being fearless: if it "needed" to be said, I was up for the task. Sign me up for any controversy as a literal relationship mercenary. And I'm not alone in this. We've all met the person who professes, with some flair, that they "just say what's on their mind" or they "just call it as they see it." Or even the gutless wonder who's quite practiced at throwing a verbal grenade and walking (running) in the other direction as it explodes and damages someone's self-confidence, self-esteem, or disintegrates the trust and collaboration of a team.

Often the distinction between being fearless and reckless is a very fine line—so fine that we either don't see it, or minimize the consequences if we step over it—especially if we can justify it as being harmless to others. But we often forget to include ourselves in that equation: *How do my actions align with or violate my deeper values and purpose in life? What's the price I'm paying for doing so?*

With Seth's wise counsel forever lodged in my head, I can report that I'm improving on being more deliberate, more intentional, and more calibrated with what I do, what I buy, and what

I say. I've also come to better confront which parts of my personality are endearing and valuable to others and which parts . . . aren't. My wife recently told me (after listening to me on countless conference calls, Zoom calls, and other virtual meetings) that much of my humor is based on making fun of other people—sometimes quite harshly. After months of pandemic-related quarantine and being subjected to hundreds of my calls, she sadly wasn't making this up. Her insight came as a bit of a shock, as I've often thought of myself as a "teaser" (also known to some linguistic experts as a "jerk"). But with some reflection and self-analysis, it was easier to see where I crossed the line from being fearless to reckless. By the way, notice that my wife was being fearless in her feedback (she risked offending me to help me) versus me being reckless (see how witty and funny I am at your expense?).

Acting fearlessly requires us to show courage and move outside our normal comfort zone as we contemplate the consequences of our words and actions. If I say exactly what's on my mind, in the heat of the moment, what will our relationship look and feel like next week? If I overcommit and agree to a partnership or an alliance and then get bored—or worse, just change my mind later—how will that impact my reputation?

I watched Seth act fearlessly several years ago while on a winter ski vacation in Park City, Utah. Seth, at my invitation, agreed to join FranklinCovey's executive team and CEO at his home and meet for a few hours to explore some areas of potential partnership. Like many first-time face-to-face meetings, the agenda was a bit too fluid and organic, and nothing clear was developing out of our conversations. Then Seth, who's a self-proclaimed iconoclast, made a polite yet bold declaration about the areas he was most certainly not interested in pursuing, and one that he might be. Gracious but firm; concise but clear. Both efficient and effective, as is Seth's hallmark.

For Seth, I'm guessing it would have been reckless to portray interest in any collaboration, partnership, or opportunity where he didn't clearly see it aligning with his own purpose and mission. Similarly, he also strikes me as the type of entrepreneur and leader who loves placing bets, taking calibrated risks, and trying new things—provided they are aligned to his own deliberate priorities. He knows how to delicately balance the line between fearless and reckless.

Like most things in life, differentiating between being fearless and reckless begins with self-awareness: our ability to understand who we are, who we want to be, and what it's like to be in a meeting with us, work on a project with us, join a video conference with us, be in a friendship or romantic relationship with us, and so on. Don't allow being fearless to mask the slippery slope that quickly leads to becoming reckless. Stay true to being fearless when it serves a higher purpose.

. . .

THE TRANSFORMATIONAL INSIGHT

Create a heightened understanding of when your fearlessness impacts people beyond yourself and results in diminishing them and even your mutual relationship.

THE QUESTION

When you find yourself confusing these two concepts, ask yourself, *How do I want to show up? How do I want to be remembered? How do I want to make the other person feel?*

TODD DAVIS

FRANKLINCOVEY
ONLEADERSHIP
WITH SCOTT MILLER

EPISODE 3

TODD DAVIS
THE POWER OF RELATIONSHIPS

Every organization has a linchpin—the single person every employee looks to as their inspiration and model of their own potential, the calm in the storm, and the leader who candidly sets the standard. Sometimes it's the founder or namesake. Other times it's the CEO or board chair. Perhaps it's the face of the firm, the figurehead, or someone who has the longest tenure and unparalleled institutional knowledge. It's different for every organization.

For FranklinCovey, it's our Chief People Officer, Todd Davis.

I'm sure some associates, with no disrespect to Todd, disagree with me and say it's our CEO or perhaps one of our cofounders. But the one benefit from being the author is it's my book and I can write what I want (as long as it's not libelous).

You may recognize Todd's name. He's a well-known thought leader and has keynoted hundreds of events, including the prestigious World Business Forum and many human resource and professional-development conferences. Todd is the two-time *Wall Street Journal* bestselling author of *Get Better: 15 Proven Practices to Building Effective Relationships at Work*, and coauthor of *Everyone Deserves a Great Manager: The 6 Critical Practices for Leading a Team* with Victoria Roos-Olsson and me. Todd also appears frequently on podcasts, radio interviews, and in columns and articles about workplace culture and relationships. Oh yeah, almost forgot: for his day job, he serves as the Executive Vice President and Chief People Officer, leading our culture, recruiting efforts, employment policies, professional development, and countless other vital areas that end up in People Services or Human Resources. Todd also has been instrumental in the design, development, and delivery of many of our bestselling solutions. I find it most telling that Todd still facilitates our foundational personal-development work session, *The 7 Habits of Highly Effective People,* internally to our associates. Increasingly, the cobbler's kids *do in fact* have shoes, at least at FranklinCovey!

Todd is fiercely focused on building relationships at every turn. In fact, that's a word you will hear and see frequently in his speaking, writing, and interviews—relationships—because Todd will tell you they're really all that matters if you want results.

Todd has somewhat laid down the proverbial gauntlet and declares in his first book, *Get Better,* that the adage "People are an organization's most valuable asset" is not true. In fact, it's bunk. Todd isn't discounting the value of people in any company or institution; he's merely challenging the idea that people are an organization's most valuable asset. Todd takes it a full step further and evangelizes that it's the relationships *between* those people that matters most, and that's the transformational insight of this chapter.

The relationships of your people build your culture, and together they form your ultimate competitive advantage. What you insist are the key differentiators are no longer, and everything can, and is, being copied or stolen from your organization—your patents and trademarks, logo, supply chain, pricing, go-to-market strategy, and more. They may feel unique to you, but that's a fantasy in the long run. Your only truly unique assets are the relationships between your people, which creates your culture. And they're inextricably linked.

Thus, building authentic, high-trust relationships should be an obsession of every leader.

Now, you might think, *Wait, Scott, you previously wrote that one of my main roles as a leader is to recruit and retain talented people.* Yep, that's right. It is. But you can't simply stop there. Because if all you do is hire and keep wunderkinds, you'll have a group of talented individual contributors all operating independently of each other.

Super, but that's the sport known as golf. (Is it really a sport?)

Beyond the incredibly challenging and vital role of recruiting and retaining quality talent is ensuring that talent is collaborating, communicating, sharing, and complementing each other—that they're apologizing, forgiving, and perhaps most importantly, pre-forgiving one another. Because even the most mature, well-educated, sophisticated, and talented associates say and do stupid stuff to others. It's called being human. And, perhaps frustratingly, all your associates are human—at least for a few more years until AI disrupts that.

In the book Todd, Victoria, and I wrote, *Everyone Deserves a Great Manager*, we share six critical practices for leading a team. They are:

1. Develop a leader's mindset.

2. Hold regular one-on-ones.

3. Set up your team to get results.

4. Create a culture of feedback.

5. Lead your team through change.

6. Manage your time and energy.

I mention these because the first practice is an imperative precursor to Todd's premise about relationships. Pour yourself a cocktail while I expound on this.

When you develop a leader's mindset, you challenge your own deeply entrenched paradigms and beliefs—about your team members, your leadership style, and what your role is and isn't. An effective leadership mindset is that you achieve results *with* and *through* other people. Let that sink in.

I'll write it again because it's absolutely transformational. A leader's mindset and contribution is to achieve results *with* and *through* other people.

When you as a leader embrace this new effective mindset, everything changes and improves as you begin (or recommit) to not only putting your people first but focusing on the relationships between you and your team members. You also begin to pay attention to how you can help build better, more trusting relationships across your division and organization. As a result, you see your role differently. No longer do you have the urge or need to rush in and save the day. Gone is the outdated mindset "If you want it done right, do it yourself." Instead, you realize that your key role and primary contribution is to build capabilities and capacity in others. You slow down, become more patient, and start listening, coaching, and mentoring others so they can learn and grow. It's tangible, and the results become evident immediately.

This new mindset may require a change in you—not only in how you think and what you believe (about yourself and others) but how you behave. Achieving results with and through others may well require you to become a transition figure in your culture, saying no to the constant urgencies coming your way that prevent you from investing the time in teaching others. That often means resisting the validation that comes from solving an issue or a problem yourself because it's just faster and easier.

Look around and inventory the health of your relationships at work. And while you're at it, in your nonwork life as well. When you come to believe that's what is most valuable in life, everything gets better.

. . .

THE TRANSFORMATIONAL INSIGHT

Resist falling into the trap of believing that your organization's most valuable asset is the collection of your people. Your most valuable asset is your *culture*, built and defined by the relationships *between* your people.

THE QUESTION

Confront reality. Are you just repeating what sounds convenient regarding the power of relationships, or do you truly believe and act in a way that supports their value in your organization and overall life?

DONALD MILLER

FRANKLINCOVEY
ONLEADERSHIP
WITH SCOTT MILLER

EPISODE 59

DONALD MILLER
CLARIFY YOUR MESSAGE

The Rocky Horror Picture Show
Christopher Guest
String Cheese Incident
Casamigos Tequila
Jennifer Coolidge
Jai Alai
Donald Miller

WHAT DOES THIS list have in common? They all have a cult following. Okay, I acknowledge it's the first time in history that Donald Miller has been on the same list as the band String Cheese Incident or the sport jai alai (pronounced hi-lie), but I aim to surprise people!

I feel like Donald Miller burst on the scene within the past few years, but as you read in chapter sixteen featuring Nely Galán, overnight fame ain't a thing—unless your name is Lorena Bobbitt. (Factually, overnight fame is a thing, just not to be confused with overnight success. They're distinctly different.)

Donald Miller is the author of the massively influential book *Building a Story Brand: Clarify Your Message So Customers Will Listen*. He's also authored multiple other bestsellers including *Blue Like Jazz*, *Marketing Made Simple,* and the recently released *Business Made Simple.* He's the CEO of StoryBrand, a marketing and messaging consulting firm in Nashville, Tennessee, and is the cohost of the *Building a StoryBrand* podcast. (Perhaps there's some foreshadowing in how often he repeats the business name and what it does for its clients.)

Stay tuned for that lesson.

As a top ten marketing podcast on iTunes, *StoryBrand* is insanely valuable for anybody, in any industry, looking to build their brand, clarify their messaging, and increase their revenue. Donald doesn't know this, but serendipitously, he's partially responsible for building my own brand as a writer, speaker, and career coach. I was fortunate to be a guest on his podcast when my first book, *Management Mess to Leadership Success,* launched, and it just so happened that Rachel Hollis, who's apparently part of Donald's cult following, heard the interview, bought my book on Amazon, and the next thing I know, she's holding my book up on her own Facebook live series and it's exploding in sales. Fast-forward ten minutes and I receive a LinkedIn InMail from Rachel Hollis asking me if I'd come down to her office in Austin and share some leadership insights with her and her team. Then I'm onstage a few weeks later at her RISE Business event in Charleston, South Carolina, in front of seven thousand people and, as they say, the rest is history.

Insane. Thank you, Donald. Thank you, Rachel. I will never forget you or the platform both of you provided me.

So, about six months later, I invited Donald Miller to appear on FranklinCovey's *On Leadership* podcast. It was a captivating conversation, and as the CMO at the time, I was riveted listening and learning about our own firm's messaging challenges. I recommend you listen to the interview—he's a master at his craft.

Donald's "ten thousand hours" have built his following as an expert on clarifying your organization's messaging strategy, which typically requires a conscious shift—a struggle for most—to move off your own story and create one where others can see themselves in it. Simply, Donald teaches that many struggling businesses have great people working in them and solid business strategies, but their self-serving messaging is getting in the way of building a brand customers want to care about. Donald follows the timeless "Hero's Journey" story format to help clients discover and answer: Who are we? Who is our customer? And how do we invite them into a story that helps them win?

He shares an example in our interview of superb messaging that I can't seem to shake, likely because of the source. It begins with the 2016 presidential election between Donald Trump, Hillary Clinton, and—to be fair I should include at least one of the write-in candidates I saw reported in the press—Giant Meteor.

Reflecting on the 2016 election, Donald Miller said, "A simple message about the betterment of the customer is always going to beat the simple messaging of how we are great as a brand. This mindset shift requires you to move outside your ego, your journey, your story, your reason, and shift to your customer's ego, their journey, their story, their reason. . . . Your key to all messaging and marketing is to associate your products with the survival of your customer and do so in such simple, easy language that nobody has to burn any calories to understand it."

Donald (not the candidate) has traveled the entire country asking thousands of people, "What did Jeb Bush want to do with

America?" Nobody knows. Donald's never received an answer from anyone he's spoken to. But then, when he asks, "What did Donald Trump want to do with America?" They say, "Make America Great Again."

Regardless of your politics, move past them and absorb what Donald Miller is telling us: a simple message will beat a complicated one nearly every time.

What did Hillary Clinton want to do with America? Nobody knows. Her messaging was "I'm with her." Perhaps it should have been, "She's with you." At least that would have reorientated the messaging toward the customer (voter).

Simply put, no calorie-burning messaging. Donald Miller proposes that's what Donald Trump did in the 2016 election and Hillary Clinton didn't.

Neither of us is suggesting that's the sole reason Donald Trump became president. But it certainly helped. Donald Miller enlightens us that we're bombarded each day with over three thousand marketing messages; and yours, if it's like most, is "like a cat chasing a rat in a windchime factory." This chapter is not a discourse on a winning political strategy, but rather to share the transformational insight on ensuring that your message focuses less on you and more on your customer.

Begin the difficult, even painful work to flip the script from your journey to your customer's journey. If your customer does not see themself in your messaging, you're completely wasting their time and yours. Too many business owners and marketing professionals feel compelled to talk about things near and dear to their own journey: Why our grandfather founded the business. How much money we've invested in research and development. What our unique approach is to the marketplace. The fact that our global coverage is second to none.

Save it all for your sales conference. Share none of it with your customers unless they ask. Instead, deliberately focus your messaging such that the customer can see themself in it in plainly spoken, simple language they understand and can identify with.

The customer cares about arriving safely at *their* destination, not how *you* got to *yours*.

. . .

THE TRANSFORMATIONAL INSIGHT

If your customer cannot find themself squarely in your messaging, it's frankly useless—for both of you.

THE QUESTION

It likely feels counterintuitive, but are you capable of putting your business needs aside when creating your messaging—to bring your client's business needs front and center?

M.J. FIÈVRE

FRANKLINCOVEY
ONLEADERSHIP
WITH SCOTT MILLER

EPISODE 124

M.J. FIÈVRE

BALANCING EFFICIENCY WITH EFFECTIVENESS

Being highly efficient, while laudable in many circumstances, is by itself unlikely to raise someone to a level worthy of inclusion as a Master Mentor. Admittedly, efficiency is a topic I know well—probably too well (more on that in a moment). There are, thankfully, those who go beyond just efficiency to become, what our firm's cofounder Dr. Stephen R. Covey termed, a highly *effective* person. Michele Jessica Fièvre (rhymes with Kiev), known colloquially as M.J., is exactly that. And with all deference to M.J., I recognize the inherent awkwardness in being called out as a model for a book that's sold forty million copies worldwide and was the impetus behind our global leadership firm. M.J.'s transformational insight comes not only from how she practices effectiveness in her life today, but in the remarkable journey of where her life began.

Ever been to St. Barts? Antigua? Puerto Rico or any of the US or British Virgin Islands? Then you know the Caribbean is stunning and a magnet for vacationers, second homeowners, and those who have coasted into the sunset of their life. The countries are a magical draw for millions of tourists, including me, and even seem to have a restorative power for me when I've visited. Someday when I grow up to become rich and famous (clock is ticking, people, I'm fifty-three), I'll own a second home there. It's a beautiful part of the world and continues to thrive despite occasional setbacks from Mother Nature.

And then there's Haiti.

Sharing the island known as Hispaniola with the Dominican Republic, Haiti can't seem to catch a break. Enduring centuries of despotic rulers, dictators, corrupt presidents, systemic poverty, devastating earthquakes, and no significant natural resources to support its economy, this Caribbean country, rich in culture and lovely people, is also known as the poorest country in the Western Hemisphere. Its literacy rate hovers around 60 percent compared to most of its neighbors' 90 percent, and the future isn't looking very bright, despite the efforts of many celebrities and former US presidents dedicated to changing its trajectory. Haiti isn't exactly what I could call a trampoline for success. And yet, this is where Michele Jessica Fièvre bounded from to land where she is today.

Like nearly all of her Haitian neighbors, schoolmates, and friends, poverty, crime, and desperation surrounded M.J. and her family. Although her parents were both educated professionals, there was no shortage of abuse in her home and upbringing. I won't expand on that, except to say she and her sisters became determined to rise up and out before they were in middle school.

M.J. immigrated to the United States in her early twenties, and through a tireless work ethic and insatiable quest for learning, rose to become a senior editor at Mango, the nation's fastest-growing independent book publisher. As an author herself, M.J. has written sixteen books, eight in French and eight in English. Her many bestselling books keep her constantly booked as a podcast guest and an in-demand keynote speaker. M.J. speaks four languages and has translated many books as a result of that talent. For some context . . . I've barely mastered simple conversational Spanish, and I come from a land where opportunity trampolines abound!

M.J.'s books consistently debut at #1 on numerous Amazon.com lists, and you may know some of her titles including *Badass Black Girl*, *Empowered Black Girl*, and *Black, Brave, Beautiful*. She attributes much of her success to her voracious reading as a child, and even taught herself English through American books. I have three boys and I adore them and their emerging talents, but none of them are close to mastering a foreign language, self-taught, through reading alone.

At twelve, M.J. found a copy of *The 7 Habits of Highly Effective People*, and she will tell you it inspired her to search for a level of effectiveness that was perhaps unrecognizable to her extended family and friends, and likely unfathomable to members of her town and country. For those few of you who may not have read it yet, here's a short primer:

Habit 1: Be Proactive. Being proactive means more than taking the initiative; it means we don't blame circumstances, conditions, or conditioning for our behavior.

Habit 2: Begin with the End in Mind. Beginning with the end in mind means understanding and visualizing our destination so that the steps we take are always in the right direction.

Habit 3: Put First Things First. Putting first things first means employing the judgment to differentiate between the urgent and important tasks that flow from Habits 1 and 2.

Habit 4: Think Win-Win. Thinking win-win is the framing of one's heart and mind to seek mutual benefit and satisfaction in our interactions with others.

Habit 5: Seek First to Understand, Then to Be Understood. Seeking first to understand and then to be understood means to diagnose before you prescribe—to listen with empathy to understand the other person.

Habit 6: Synergize. To synergize is to embrace the principle that *the whole is greater than the sum of its parts* by building high levels of trust and cooperation, and celebrating differences with others.

Habit 7: Sharpen the Saw. Sharpening the saw means exercising and renewing the four dimensions of our nature: our physical, social/emotional, mental, and spiritual selves.

These habits, when collectively modeled, make us highly effective. But many people wrongly refer to the book as *The 7 Habits of Highly Efficient People*. There's a significant distinction between being simply efficient versus being effective, which is the transformational insight M.J. understands and illustrates in every interaction I've had with her.

Enter the poster boy for efficiency: Scott Jeffrey Miller.

I am a self-proclaimed world-class model of efficiency. Simply put, I get sh*t done. In fact, my propensity to get sh*t done has arguably been the biggest contributor to any professional success I've achieved in life. My efficiency, also known to many as productivity, has been the hallmark of my brand for both good and bad.

I am an insanely hard worker and love to think big and deliver even bigger. I wake at 4:00 a.m. most days and begin writing my weekly column for Inc.com, *Utah Business* magazine, or many blog posts, articles, or other requests that may have come in from my publicist that week. I host a global leadership podcast; I am concurrently authoring four significant books and delivering keynotes to multiple clients; and I own a thriving career-coaching and consulting business. I serve as a senior advisor on Thought Leadership for FranklinCovey and in that capacity lead a team of ten associates. I speak with numerous people each week offering them coaching on their brands, businesses, and other items. Basically, if you call me, I'll help you.

Add to the above list "husband," "father to three boys," "brother," "son," and "that annoying neighbor who's up at 5:00 a.m. on Saturdays," showered, dressed, and at the local nursery buying flowers at 6:00 a.m. They're planted by 7:00 a.m., the lawn is raked and mowed by 8:30 a.m., the car washed by 9:00 a.m., and I'm at my tennis game an hour later. All that, and my day has just begun! Fast. Quick. Check it off my task list and move to the next. And Sundays make my Saturdays look lazy.

Exhausted yet? I left most of the details out so you would believe me. I am an insanely productive person who has mastered the art of efficiency. Often, the best way to examine something is to contrast it with something else. And since I haven't been deluged with folks raising their hands and volunteering to be a counterexample, bear with me.

My efficiency, as I suspect you can already guess, tends to work against me as well. And when I say *tends*, I mean *absolutely without exception* works against me. When my supercharged efficiency moves into my relationships and I treat people like I'm cleaning up the kitchen after dinner or managing my email inbox, I pay a price. And sadly, so do they. As I rush through conversations, meetings, video conference calls, performance reviews, and coaching interactions, few people in my life ever feel listened to, understood, or validated. Nearly all of them, personally and professionally, feel a level of anxiety because of the personal brand I've built with them—Scott is busy, so talk fast, don't waste time, and expect little interpersonal connection. Keep it short and get to the point or Scott will move on. I'm not proud of this, but I'm painfully self-aware of it. My biggest strength is, surprise, also my biggest liability.

In the wise words of Dr. Stephen R. Covey, "With people, fast is slow and slow is fast." You cannot be efficient with people; it simply doesn't work. You must choose to be effective with people. If you want to build high trust, mutually beneficial relationships—the lifeblood of every culture, organization, and family—it's vital to slow down. To genuinely learn and demonstrate effectiveness, you must listen with empathy by checking into the other person's pain or passion. Some questions I ground myself in when I'm tempted to move into efficiency with people are: How do I want to show up in this conversation? How do I want to be remembered? How do I want this person to feel treated and valued by me? Besides holding this mindset, being effective also means I need to turn off my phone, shut my laptop, and authentically and genuinely "check in."

As you can see in my push for efficiency, I can become highly ineffective if I fall victim to my natural tendencies with relationships—which in life is all that really matters.

Enter the poster girl for effectiveness: M.J. Fièvre.

Now, before I explain more, don't for a moment think M.J. lacks efficiency and productivity. Just revisit my opening description of her and you realize she's nailed the efficiency side of things: editor, author, podcaster, speaker, business owner, spouse, daughter, sister, and friend. M.J. has a work ethic like no other.

What's different about M.J. is what it's like to work with her. I'd describe it as calm, pleasant, inspiring, comforting even. Her voice level, patience, and listening skills are my all-consuming envy. M.J. truly values people, diverse perspectives, and rigorous debate—the collective outcome of all of that which is a leadership style that drives inclusion, validation, and quality results. Additionally, she brings a genuine level of safety and amity that I aspire to. If I am the "Puree" setting on a blender, M.J. is "Gently Fold." If I'm "Fast Wash" on the washing machine, M.J. is "Delicates."

M.J. has mastered the skill of when to be efficient without compromising being highly effective. Some of it may be her natural personality, but I believe it's a learned habit. M.J. intentionally chooses when to be efficient on projects, tasks, and initiatives that don't require interpersonal collaboration. Likewise, she exercises trust, care, empathy, patience, and understanding for those that do. She slows down significantly when needed, and as a result, achieves a heightened level of clarity among those involved in the discussion or project. People working with M.J. feel heard, valued, and understood. Ironically, productivity isn't slowed—it's actually quickened.

Highly effective people like M.J. build an intuition for how, where, and when to balance the necessity of efficiency with being effective. It doesn't come overnight, and for many of us, it's not natural. But with this awareness of the difference between efficiency and effectiveness, all of us can replicate M.J.'s influence.

There's an interesting twist to M.J.'s story. We started with her as a twelve-year-old girl living in Haiti, first reading *The 7 Habits of Highly Effective People* and contemplating how to implement it into her life. Fast-forward twenty years or so and M.J., through her role at Mango Publishing, was asked to be the editor for FranklinCovey's *The 7 Habits Guided Journal.* Annie Oswald, who is a thirty-year associate of FranklinCovey and serves as the vice president of our Media Publishing group, selected M.J. to write the introduction based on her passion for the content, but also because our organization viewed her as an aspiring model for all of us. This was long before she was a guest on our podcast series or I envisioned writing this book, featuring her as a Master Mentor. Who would have thought a Creole-speaking girl from Haiti would one day be writing the English foreword to a global blockbuster book she read as a preteen?

I have a suspicion M.J. wouldn't have ruled it out—all to what would have been the delight of Dr. Covey, had he lived to see his work come full circle in her.

. . .

THE TRANSFORMATIONAL INSIGHT

Be mindful that even a strength such as efficiency in tasks can be a weakness if not bridged into effectiveness in relationships.

THE QUESTION

Have you folded your relationships into your to-do list, then hit the "Puree" button?

WHITNEY JOHNSON

FRANKLINCOVEY
ONLEADERSHIP
WITH SCOTT MILLER

EPISODE 41

WHITNEY JOHNSON
DISRUPT YOURSELF

You've likely noticed that throughout *Master Mentors*, I reference a slew of books, colleagues, and advisors beyond those featured as one of the thirty Master Mentors mentioned. That's because throughout my career, and to the extent I've achieved any success, the wisdom and coaching I've received from others has been abundant and instrumental. I could write an entire bonus chapter about the personal mentors in my life who haven't been on the podcast, but their insights were just as transformational for me. One such person—referenced more than once in this book—is Judy Henrichs.

Judy is a communication advisor to executives, and after a wildly successful career at FranklinCovey as a consultant, she pursued her dream of opening a Montessori school in her hometown just outside of St. Louis. She continues to coach me in my public-speaking skills, and among the many bits of wisdom she's imparted to me over twenty years is this little ditty: "There comes a time in everyone's career when you've given 90 percent of what you have to offer your organization, and you've also taken from them 90 percent of what they have to offer you; and frankly, the last 10 percent, either way, may just not be worth the effort." I've repeated this nugget of wisdom to people so many times, I've lost count.

Chew on that while I introduce a new Master Mentor, Whitney Johnson.

Whitney's many accomplishments include being a bestselling author, renowned strategy advisor and coach, podcaster, and keynote speaker. She is also one of the fifty leading business thinkers in the world, as named by Thinkers 50, and was named a Top 15 Coach from Marshall Goldsmith out of sixteen thousand applicants. Her books include *Build an A-Team* and *Disrupt Yourself*. As you're likely learning about me, I love adages, quotes, and quips, and one of my all-time favorites is: "Act or be acted upon."

That sentiment is the essence of *Disrupt Yourself*. Whitney argues that in our careers, we can learn from the greatest disrupters in business and industry. We should lead the disruption in our professional lives and thus avoid the inevitable disruption constantly headed our way and foisted on us by others. Whitney suggests we envision our careers as a series of ladders, and when we reach the top of one, we jump over to the bottom of another, continually gaining upward traction. I absolutely love this metaphor and think it's vital as we look at our long-term career trajectories.

Too many of us don't lead our own careers, instead leaving them to chance or to the direction of others. One of the most depressing but also motivating quotes I've ever heard is from a fellow executive: "You're never in the room when your career is decided for you." Sad but true for far too many. That's why the concept of disrupting yourself before you're disrupted by outside forces is an imperative Whitney speaks so passionately about. Naturally, disrupting yourself means different strategies for each of us based on our individual circumstances.

I'm not so naive to think each of us can just up and quit our job every time we need to scratch a professional itch. I also know many colleagues who've lost their jobs and were caught completely by surprise. Further, they took it immensely personally. It crushed their self-esteem and self-confidence. Here's a sidebar tip you should never forget: your job is a career; it's not your life. I have authored books on careers, I host a career-coaching series on my website, and I speak about career strategies frequently on radio and podcast interviews, but I'm very aware that my career needs to be a narrow place in my life. It's merely a means to an end—certainly not the end. Be sure to take stock of how much of your life is focused on your career and recalibrate as necessary.

So, how do you know if you should self-disrupt? The answer is in what Whitney calls the S Curve of Disruption. This theory, which first took form in the 1960s, describes how quickly products might be adopted by consumers. Picture a giant S, tilted slightly to the right to look more like a roller coaster. All careers start at the bottom left and move through the S configuration. In the early days of any new role, learning can feel like a slow slog (see Figure 2).

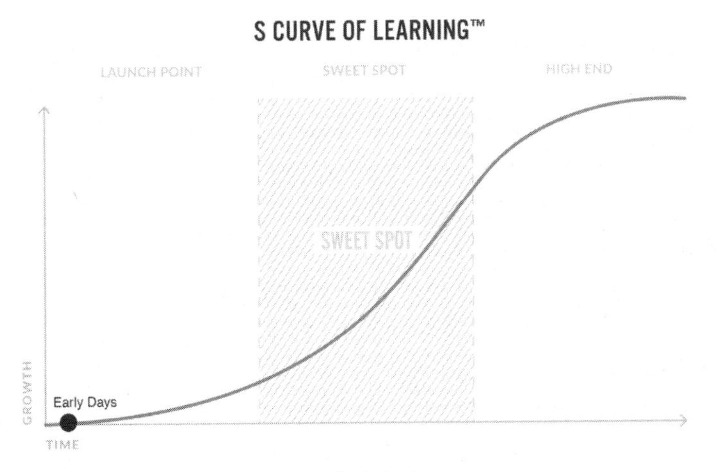

FIGURE 2

Fast-forward six-ish months, and you should be feeling more confident and competent. Then, as you move up to the top of the S curve—perhaps two to three years in your role—you may find you're no longer challenged (see Figure 3). You might have even become a bit intellectually lazy because you're no longer experiencing what Whitney calls "the feel-good effects of learning."

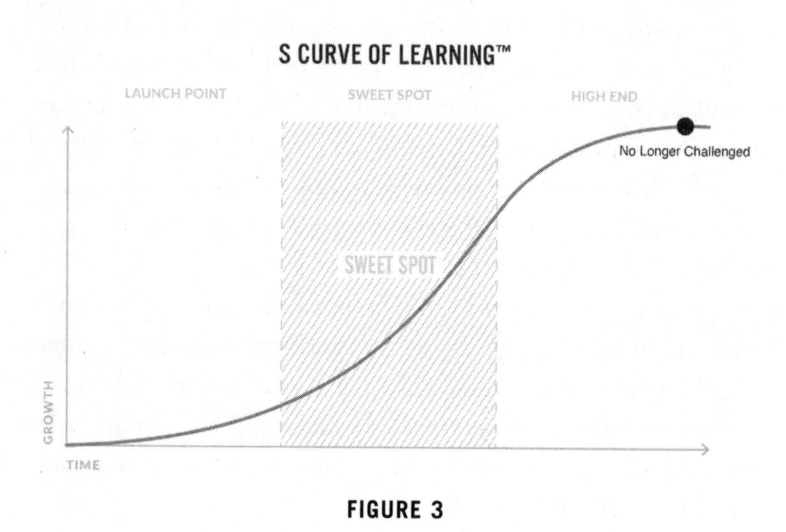

FIGURE 3

It's at this point that many of us underperform, not even realizing we're contributing to our own professional demise. Candidly, we're bored, and it's time to move to the bottom of a new S curve and continue through another round along your professional journey. But few of us acknowledge, or are even aware, when this is happening, exposing ourselves to being disrupted by any number of outside forces including Human Resources because the Chief Financial Officer is eyeing your role as part of a cost-cutting measure.

Act or be acted upon.

Let's identify the telltale sign that it's time for self-disruption. Whitney suggests that at about the three-year mark in any role, we become restless, whether or not we recognize it. For some of us, it's longer, like four to six years. But just because we've hit one of those milestones doesn't mean we automatically quit. If you're still engaged and learning, then it may not be time to move on. Different strokes for different folks. Take a moment and think back on your own career journey and see if it hits home.

This insight nailed my own career journey at FranklinCovey. At the time of this writing, I've thrived for twenty-five years in the firm. Technically, at age fifty-three, I'm a Gen Xer, so this length of tenure is rare for my generation. My generation's tenure and loyalty to an organization is certainly less than that of the Boomers and Traditionalists before us (my father worked for his employer for thirty-two years . . . before he was disrupted and let go).

Conversely, recent research shows that members of Gen Y and Gen Z have significantly shorter tenures, with the far end being thirty-six months in a single role or career, and the mean closer to eighteen to twenty-four months. In no way is this a judgment of one generation's staying power over another—just an assessment. Offended or disagree? Look at a hundred resumes from this generation compared to others, and you'll be converted. Future careers look shorter because options are more plentiful, and our sense of what a necessary education must look like is also being massively disrupted. Consider the sharing economy, and it's going to be a whole new world for future careers.

I've been privileged to have entered and exited eight distinct careers in the past twenty-five years, all at FranklinCovey. Do the math, and you'll see I line up almost exactly with Whitney's insight of the three-year average per role. Not every organization can recruit and retain talent like FranklinCovey has, but perhaps it's an insight that, as a leader, you should think about. Can your organization address your ability to create a culture where your current employees fulfill more of their overall career journeys inside your company? For many organizations and employers, retention is a key metric on many fronts, and I suggest it's a measure by which every leader should be judged.

It takes enormous courage to disrupt yourself, but I've found the most engaged and satisfied professionals become experts at it. I can personally attest to that.

. . .

THE TRANSFORMATIONAL INSIGHT

Exercise the boldness to understand where you are on your career journey and when it's time to disrupt yourself before you are inevitably disrupted by external forces or people.

THE QUESTION

Where are you on your own three-year itch? Are you confident and competent enough to disrupt yourself and step over to the next ladder before it disappears? Are there skills you need to develop to become relevant and valuable enough to stick the landing?

TRENT SHELTON

FRANKLINCOVEY
ONLEADERSHIP
WITH SCOTT MILLER

EPISODE 114

TRENT SHELTON
THE POWER PERSPECTIVE

Baseball. Basketball. Football. He didn't really care which one—he just wanted to be a professional athlete. From an early age, this was Trent Shelton's dream. And he accomplished it as a wide receiver for the Indianapolis Colts. And the Seattle Seahawks . . . well, almost (more on that later).

Trent is the author of several books, including *The Greatest You* and *Straight Up*. Both are raw and real accounts of his own journey in life and the mindset he's become known for—moving from a prison perspective to a power perspective. Trent is a frequent speaker at conferences and events, and perhaps is best known as a leading social media personality with an audience of fifty million. His *On Leadership* interview was captivating, and I am going to dedicate this chapter to re-creating his story as closely as possible, as I think it will be profound for many.

Although his real love was baseball, Trent was more talented at football and earned a scholarship to Baylor University in Texas.

After a standout career in college, Trent was certain he'd be a top draft pick—at least by the fourth or fifth round. But that didn't happen. Instead, he was picked up as an undrafted free agent by the Colts for a year before being cut—fired, for those not familiar with football terms. He spent some time with the Washington Redskins (now known as the Washington Football Team) and, once out of the NFL, suited up for the Arena Football League's Tulsa Talons. But his real insight came between stints with the Colts and Redskins when he landed a position on the Seattle Seahawks practice squad. This was a dream fulfilled. What follows, specifically about his time with the Seahawks, is best told in Trent's own words (with some minor editing for print). Similar to the chapter dedicated to Kim Scott's story at Google, I've placed a portion of the *On Leadership* interview below. I think you'll find it as invaluable as I have:

SCOTT MILLER: One of the reasons I invited you on today is because we share a passion, which is the power of vulnerability. I think one of my best currencies is talking very openly around my struggles, my challenges, and helping other people do the same. Your book is very vulnerable. You share in the first opening chapters this story that one day you are literally on the Indianapolis Colts field, and then the next you're in your parents' home in the bedroom where you were raised. You also share the knee-jerk back-and-forth between the Seahawks. Will you re-create the story of you literally headed to the airport to join the Seahawks, and what happens?

TRENT SHELTON: It's funny: I can laugh about it now. It was 2008. I was on the Seahawks practice squad and I was living in Seattle, and if you know the NFL, you know, first of all, NFL stands for "Not For Long." Also, it's a business, a numbers game. They might release you to bring in someone else, someone gets injured—it's a whole bunch of things; many variables go into it. And so, that year, I got released two times, but it might have just been for a week or so. So I decide I'll just stay up in Seattle and they'll bring me back the next week because they really like me. But this time, I got released what felt like for good.

So I was back home in Texas; I was actually in Dallas. And if you're in the Dallas–Fort Worth area, you know, it's two separate cities. So I was in Dallas. My home is in Fort Worth. I get a call from a 206 number, which is the Seattle area code. And I pick it up and they're like, "Hey, we want to bring you back." So I'm excited. So I'm already on Facebook telling everybody, I'm going back to Seattle—I'm texting my mom, my dad, and my friends and the phone rings again. It's the Seahawks; they want me to come back tonight. And there was a late flight from Dallas, but all my things are in Fort Worth.

I listen more and they say, "We don't care how you got to get here—go home, put a few clothes in a bag, go to the airport." So I hung up the phone, left my dinner, rushed home, took a little travel bag and put some things in it. I'm super excited thinking, *Man, I'm finally getting my opportunity again. I'm going to make the most out of it.*

So I'm driving to the airport, happy, park the car, get out my car. I'm actually just about to check in—like I'm walking toward the terminal and I get another call. And it was a 206 number, but it was a different number. So I answer, "Who is this?" I'm thinking maybe somebody in Seattle.

They ask, "Is this Trent?"

And I was like, "Yeah."

"Have you left yet? This is the Seattle Seahawks' personnel division. Have you left yet?"

And I was like, "No, I haven't left. What's up?"

They said, "Don't leave. We've changed our mind." And so, obviously, they said it a little bit more nicely than that, but that was the overall gist of it. And at that moment was when I hit my rock bottom. At that moment, I didn't love the game anymore. At that moment, I felt like I lost everything because I felt like that was my opportunity and I was on such a high to be crumbled in that moment. I went back to my parents' house and that's when I learned how to really be depressed and really suppress things and run from my reality. So that was a breaking point in my whole journey in my NFL career.

SCOTT MILLER: There is a lot to unpack there because I can't imagine what it would be like to have had your life's goal to become an NFL player, to have made it to the Colts, to have been recruited by the Seahawks, and to be let go numerous times. And then you get a call to come back. You pack your bags and leave your dinner, go to the airport. Your dream is coming true. And it's like this emotional, intellectual, physical, you know, back-and-forth. What have you learned—now on the other side of that—that would help other people deal with similar emotional ups and downs?

TRENT SHELTON: The first thing that comes to my heart is *your current situation is not your final destination*. And it's hard to see this in the storm. And I get it because I need to tell myself in that moment that when certain doors close, it only means that better doors are about to open. And you have a choice when those moments, when those doors are closed . . . either you can say this chapter is going to be the rest of my story, or you can say, you know what, this chapter sucks. This is not fair. But, you know, how can I get over this?

Your perspective needs to be your power or your prison. And it's pretty simple. A power perspective in that moment is saying, "Listen, it didn't work out. Maybe there's something better that's going to work out. I'm just going to control what I can

> control and pray about the things that I can't." A prison perspective would be complaining, saying: "Okay, my life is over." I wouldn't be trying to push for anything else. And so in that moment, I had a little bit of a prison perspective. But then I had to snap out of it, because I knew again my son was dependent on me. I knew I couldn't just not move. I had to do something.
>
> So I would tell you to just remember those words. Just because you have some bad chapters doesn't mean your story can't end well, and always know there's going to be a next chapter in life. So you have to be willing to adjust. You have to be willing to learn from those previous chapters and say, "You know what? I'm going to do everything I can to make sure these next chapters of my life are better."

We're all faced with choosing either a power or prison perspective when it comes to our personal and professional lives. What makes Trent a Master Mentor is not a life's book full of NFL-highlight chapters, but how he turned the page from a life-crushing disappointment to teach, inspire, and lift others. He chose power over prison. The invitation he extends to the rest of us is to do the same.

. . .

THE TRANSFORMATIONAL INSIGHT

Harness the emotional and intellectual agility to carefully choose your response when an outside situation or influence changes beyond your control.

THE QUESTION

Can you turn the page when you (inevitably) face disappointment, unfulfilled expectations, or outright violations in your life?

BRENDON BURCHARD

FRANKLINCOVEY
ONLEADERSHIP
WITH SCOTT MILLER

EPISODE 132

BRENDON BURCHARD
PROLIFIC QUALITY OUTPUT

EVERY GENERATION HAS its list of inspiring game changers. The personal-development space is massive and accommodates an endless list of competent and charismatic influencers with their own groups of followers and fans. Then the list tightens up a bit when you raise the standard, be it numbers of books sold, size of their social media platforms, or professional and educational experience. The list tightens up more as you recognize the names, even if you haven't read their books, subscribed to their YouTube channel, or seen them onstage as the keynote at your industry's or company's annual conference.

Then some more tightening happens.

What you're left with is a small number of people. This group earns their status from their multidecade reputation for wisdom. They're often known by a singular topic each of them is obsessed with and has dedicated their career to studying and researching. They have achieved influence because they simply know what they're talking about. They don't rely on their personality, charisma, or fanning social media flames to build their brand. That's not a dis on the value or influence of social platforms. Just that some use it to create momentum and others use it to sustain it.

In this rarefied last group are names like Ken Blanchard, Oprah Winfrey, Marcus Buckingham, Brené Brown, Sir Ken Robinson, Spencer Johnson, Sheryl Sandberg, Dr. Stephen R. Covey, Hyrum Smith, and John Maxwell. Some would add Tony Robbins, Liz Wiseman, Jack Canfield, and Kim Scott. Either way, this is a prestigious group of thought leaders whose influence is globally recognized.

You don't just break into this group. You earn your way in.

Like Brendon Burchard did.

Brendon is the world's leading high-performance coach and the author of many books, including his most recent release, *High Performance Habits: How Extraordinary People Become That Way*. He is a #1 *New York Times*, #1 *USA TODAY*, and #1 *Wall Street Journal* bestselling author, and his personal-development videos have been viewed 100 million times. Brendon has numerous accolades to his name—from being one of the Top 100 Most Followed Public Figures on Facebook to hosting the most watched self-help show on YouTube. Oprah named him "one of the most successful online trainers in history," perhaps because nearly two million people have taken his courses.

Brendon is legit. He's entered that stratosphere of what I like to call the "one-namers": Cher, Madonna, Oprah, Prince. Start watching for Brendon to appear on your radar and you'll see his influence and eventual inclusion in the "one-namers" club. Be patient. After all, his website is brendon.com. And no, I'm not his agent. I simply think his abundance and contribution are worth highlighting as a Master Mentor.

Brendon's most recent book, *High Performance Habits*, is extraordinary. When I interviewed him on our podcast, he told me it took him three years to write it, and he invested over a million dollars in the research to substantiate or negate the habits he would feature. The book includes many valuable insights and six habits worthy of quick review. The first three are what he calls *personal habits* and include: *seek clarity*, *generate energy*, and *raise necessity*. The final three are *social habits* and include: *increase productivity*, *develop influence*, and *demonstrate courage*. Of all the captivating content in his book and interview, what I found most transformative was a concept he coins PQO, or prolific quality output.

At issue is Brendon's dissatisfaction with the old formula of success: "Work hard; be passionate; focus on your strengths; practice a lot; stick to it; be grateful . . . so much of it is geared toward individual results and initial success. . . . But what happens after you've gotten those first wins? What happens after you have earned those grades, found some passion, gotten that job or started that dream, developed some expertise, saved some money, fallen in love, built some momentum? What helps when you want to become world-class, to lead, to create lasting impact beyond yourself?"[1]

The solution, in part, is to focus on prolific quality output. That may seem a fairly self-evident insight in its name alone, but I'll expand. Brendon is talking about the "More is not better; better is better" principle. One of the most valuable passages in the book reads, "High performers have mastered the art of prolific quality output (PQO). They produce more high-quality output than their peers over the long term, and that is *how* they become more effective, better known, more remembered. They aim their attention and consistent efforts toward PQO and minimize any distractions (including opportunities) that would steal them away from their craft."[2]

He continues to address all the distractions, including email and other projects we understandably justify. He lists a series of professional roles and what sample PQOs might look like for bloggers, sales reps, graphic designers, academics, and cupcake-store owners.

Brendon then moves into remarkable vulnerability when he turns the spotlight on himself. He describes in detail the process of when he left his role at a prestigious consulting firm, likely both running *from* something and also *to* something. He decided he wanted to build a career as a writer, a speaker, and an online trainer. Because he wasn't sure how to start, he bounced around for a full year with no clarity on which outputs really mattered to him and his future audience. Brendon describes the kind of challenges all of us can relate to if you've ever gone solo into building a business or starting a side hustle.

One day, Brendon was sitting in a café and realized, like many of us, he was confusing activity with productivity, and so wrote out his PQOs. He decided writing needed to be his key PQO, and if he were to become a recognized writer adding actual value to people, then his prolific quality output needed to become books. Consequently, Brendon has published six books at the time of this writing. He's also had success with his second and third goals: speaking and becoming an online trainer. Brendon diligently wrote out goals for each of the three categories with specific timelines and measurable deliverables. And he intensely focused his efforts on the three areas with a near obsession, saying no to any competing distraction or luring opportunity.

Brendon shares that the results in his own career are not because he's particularly special or talented (which he is) but because he honed the focus for each of the PQOs that mattered most to him. Then he gave each of the three "his obsessive attention and dedication *continuously, over the long term*." He spends 60 percent of his time weekly on writing and creating online content, and the other 40 percent on strategy, team management, customer engagement, managing social media, and so on, all of which directly or indirectly supports the first 60 percent.

His concept of identifying his PQOs is haunting me as I begin my own entrepreneurial ventures and need to stay uncharacteristically focused on the highest-leverage activities so I don't find myself, a year in, looking around and frustrated about my lack of traction.

The clock is ticking. What are your PQOs?

. . .

THE TRANSFORMATIONAL INSIGHT

It's easy to fall into the trap of measurement by volume or *quantity*. Instead, what differentiates successful and influential people is the *quality* of their output achieved through a relentless focus on the few necessary things that must get done.

THE QUESTION

Are you able to exercise the discipline to resist an array of opportunities and distractions that may validate your ego, and instead focus on the PQOs that could transform your brand?

STEPHEN M. R. COVEY

FRANKLINCOVEY
ONLEADERSHIP
WITH SCOTT MILLER

EPISODE 1

STEPHEN M. R. COVEY

PULLING THE PLUG

I WAS ONLY in my mid-twenties, but I had a dream. A very vivid dream that involved bingeing on gelatos in Rome, riding a scooter up the colorful seaside road along the Cinque Terre, and ordering pizza and wine from a Naples restaurant. Sounds pretty epic, right? And all I had to do was ascend to the "President's Club" and earn the $3,000 travel voucher. With the company about to launch a new global product to my sales portfolio, my first-ever trip to Italy was within reach.

Only it didn't happen.

It had come down to a simple but agonizing choice: pulling the plug on the launch of a new product—the highly anticipated *4 Roles of Leadership* workshop—or going forward with something that didn't meet the CEO's quality bar. To increase the pressure of that decision, the success of the offering was crucial not only to the company's brand and growth, but to the many associates whose income relied on selling and facilitating the new solution.

More importantly, there were hundreds of clients already promoting and registering participants for the new leadership offering, and delaying the launch would be painful on many fronts. Thankfully, the CEO was Stephen M. R. Covey and not Scott Jeffrey Miller. As a result, I learned a powerful lesson about the courage to pull the plug, which is this chapter's transformational insight.

In 1996, I joined Covey Leadership Center, a precursor to FranklinCovey. As the CEO of Covey Leadership Center, Stephen M. R. Covey, son of Dr. Stephen R. Covey, was a business operator long before the world came to know him as the bestselling author and renowned expert and speaker on the topics of organizational and individual trust. His first book, *The Speed of Trust: The One Thing That Changes Everything,* launched him into the global spotlight. Much of his content centers on the thirteen behaviors of high-trust leaders, and his decision to pull the plug drew on many of these: *Talk Straight*, *Right Wrongs*, *Show Loyalty*, *Deliver Results*, *Confront Reality*, *Clarify Expectations*, and *Practice Accountability.*

I was working as a commissioned, frontline sales professional at the time, and the company had spent nearly two years developing their new flagship offering, *The 4 Roles of Leadership*. I had called every current and prospective client I could think of to talk up the new leadership solution and presell it as much as possible. My goal was to contribute to a robust "out of the gate" release while simultaneously ensuring my Tuscan sun dreams.

Shortly before the global launch, to the collective shock and angst of the entire organization, Stephen pulled the plug. As a result, the organizational dominoes began to fall: sales staff complained, pay-per-day consultants suddenly had no "days" around the solution to bill, our reputation took a hit, and revenue suffered. Practically every sales associate jumped on the phone and made the painful admission to their formerly excited clients. And like the ancient city of Pompeii, my dreams of Italy turned to ash.

Although I didn't fully recognize it at the time, it took real courage for Stephen to pull the plug, despite the consequences. His assessment had been that the product lacked the gravitas, tools, and life/career-changing insights the brand had built its foundation upon.

Eight months later, the improved solution released worldwide. *The 4 Roles of Leadership* went on to a ten-plus-year run as a dominant leadership-development solution adopted by thousands of organizations and corporate universities. Stephen's instincts had been right, and the short-term pain was soon forgotten in the hindsight of the product's incredible run.

In the long run, we tend to forget any inconvenience and disruption in the wake of a delayed but, ultimately, world-class product or service. It requires extraordinary courage, discipline, and care to pull the plug. Rarely will the marketplace skewer you for raising your standard, but prepare to pay the price if your launch is all splash and no substance.

I recently drew on Stephen's lesson while serving as Franklin-Covey's Executive Vice President for Thought Leadership. In this role, I had companywide responsibility for areas including public relations and the publication of our many books, which drive the opinions and impressions tens of millions of people have of our company and brand experience. The supremely talented team that leads our book releases was coming up to a deadline on a brand-defining book and was working furiously to ensure we met the commitment. Frankly, missing it would be brutal and could even damage our relationship and reputation with a major publisher.

I planned to review the manuscript the weekend before it was due, assuming I'd have a few dozen slight edits. (I'd been peripherally involved in its development over the previous year.) I sat down at my kitchen table that Friday evening and three pages in began to worry. I didn't like the opening. Truthfully, I hated the opening. I kept reading. I didn't like most of the first chapter either. Or the second. I stopped and texted a few colleagues who'd been involved to ask their opinion. Their feedback wasn't encouraging.

I returned to the manuscript and kept reading until I couldn't continue any further. The book needed significant improvements, despite the expertise and writing prowess of the authors and support team. The next day, I called everyone together and dropped the bomb. To the team's credit, they not only agreed with my critique but began a solid month of heroic fifty- to sixty-hour weeks to restructure and resequence entire chapters. My contribution (dwarfed by theirs) was to reread the entire 280 pages with line-by-line editorial suggestions and join the daily 5:00 a.m. Zoom calls to debate the proposed changes.

So that the authors could focus solely on writing, another colleague and I committed to call the publisher and offer our *mea culpa*. We spoke for a painful ninety minutes as we walked them through our self-imposed quagmire. I'll never forget it—not because of the call's length or awkwardness, but for how appreciative the publisher was because of our complete transparency. I'd call it a "cards face-up" conversation, and although the publishing team was gracious and allowed for a new timeline, it's a call I never want to have again.

Thirty days later, we delivered the improved manuscript. I had been perplexed with how to proceed in that crucial moment when I knew the book wasn't ready; but thankfully, I'd recalled the lesson from Stephen twenty-five years earlier. His mentorship had prepared me to face a similar "pull the plug" test of my own—a test you will face sooner or later as well.

Your moment of pulling the plug may not relate to a product deadline or other time-sensitive event. It might appear beyond the calculus of sunk costs, quality shortfalls, and even personal biases and "wishful thinking." It may surface only when someone has outlived a particular role, or for that matter, their tenure with the organization. No matter the circumstances, pulling the plug requires integrity. I don't mean that others lacked integrity and you need to rush in as the principled defender to save the day, but pulling the plug requires you to step up and *own* the accountability of that decision—a decision that will often cause some degree of pain and disruption. As a Master Mentor, Stephen M. R. Covey showed me that the best leaders will make the call and pull the plug when it's the right thing to do, even against popular sentiment, a wave of momentum, or a pressing deadline. And that trip to Italy? A year later, I took three friends on an all-expenses-paid trip, thanks in no small part to my sales success with the new offering. I'm sure I raised more than one glass of *Prosecco* in Stephen's name.

. . .

THE TRANSFORMATIONAL INSIGHT

Seeing past the "fog of war" to exercise integrity in a key moment of choice may mean pulling the plug now for the longer-term win.

THE QUESTION

What's on your horizon, personally and professionally, that you need to proactively decide if you're moving forward with full conviction, or if you should pause, reassess the opportunity, and perhaps pull the plug?

NANCY DUARTE

FRANKLINCOVEY
ONLEADERSHIP
WITH SCOTT MILLER

EPISODE 18

NANCY DUARTE
THE POWERPOINT PLAGUE

I'M CURED!

And it didn't take a physician or a miracle.

It was Nancy Duarte.

Cured of what, you ask? How about the PowerPoint Plague, the Keynote Kiss of Death, the Prezi Poison Pill? Truth is, I've been saved from the whole miserable lot!

You see, Nancy Duarte is simply remarkable. As the author of multiple bestselling books, she has changed the landscape of visual communication. Like another Master Mentor, Karen Dillon, she's the author of a *Harvard Business Review* book, *HBR Guide to Persuasive Presentations*. It's superb and I also think it's a bit like asking Elton John to play the piano at the Good Friday service in the Vatican. Likely the wrong venue, despite his talent. Meaning Nancy's *HBR* book is stellar, but she released her true genius in *slide:ology*, *Resonate*, and most recently, *DataStory*. Her TED talk is riveting (like the kind you watch over and over to absorb the meaning) and her communications firm is world renowned for their work with organizations and leaders to perfect their messaging and communication strategies. The highest compliment I could pay Nancy and her team at Duarte is that FranklinCovey is a client. Our CEO and chairman, Bob Whitman, was captivated reading her book *Resonate,* and suggested we hire her for multiple projects over the years. From Bob Whitman, Nancy has an A+ rating.

Simply stated, Nancy is a geek. A data wonk. A nerd . . . with an outrageously fun and contagiously exciting and positive personality. Sound like a paradox? Yep. Which is what I think makes her so influential. She speaks many languages—and I don't mean Flemish, Russian, or Portuguese. I mean the business languages spoken by CFOs, CEOs, COOs, CMOs, and business-unit leaders, buyers, and sellers at all levels; also entrepreneurs, founders, solopreneurs, and individuals with side hustles, as well as their current, past, and future clients.

In a word, she is nearly omniscient. Okay, that was two words, but I needed to give her some breathing room with the modifier "nearly."

I wonder what word Nancy would use to describe herself. Maybe *mathematician*?

Confused by that? Read her books and you'll be amazed at how data and information drive her creativity and counsel. I've met no one like Nancy.

Can you tell I'm a fan?

Let's talk about Nancy's transformational insight for those who present for a living—and the fact is, most of us do: less on the words you use, your body language, hand gestures, eye contact, and so on (although she could probably help there too), and more on how you carefully curate what images you will use to support, clarify, and drive home your message, often delivered by millions of professionals through Microsoft's PowerPoint.

Which is one of the many reasons Microsoft cofounder Bill Gates has a net worth exceeding $130,000,000,000. In case you got lost in the zeros, that's 130 *billion*. No offense to Robert Gaskins and Dennis Austin, who created PowerPoint back in the 1980s, but I think it's a crutch for lazy professionals not willing to pay the price to master the art of verbal storytelling.

Harsh? Yep. Let me continue.

Nancy and her team at Duarte have taught me about building and delivering effective presentations—understanding the "Hero's Journey"; the mathematical arc of any story; the roles protagonists and antagonists play; the concept of "what is and what could be . . . what is and what could be."

Presentation software can be a superb tool when needed. If needed. The problem is, we tend to use it as a crutch. Nancy taught me creating your "deck" is the last part of any communication strategy. Unfortunately, the vast majority of us begin there. Breakout session at an industry conference? Annual shareholder meeting? Company's annual sales conference? Budget meeting with the CFO? We all turn to PowerPoint and open that first blank slide template that someone, somewhere, designed for us to use. What we should do instead is to ask fundamental questions like: Who is the audience? What do they have in common? What do they need to know, and what do I want them to do differently?

This is elementary, I know, but I want to reinforce the point that we often start our high-stakes presentations with designing our slides, never looking up from the computer screen to ask ourself, *Do I even need slides? If so, how many? What other visuals might be better? A card deck? A handout? A video? A poster? A banner?* Or perhaps best of all, my own ability as a powerful, credible, and knowledgeable person able to paint a narrative of what is and what could be through my storytelling skills.

The deck, if needed at all, should be the last part of any preparation, not the first.

I'm Catholic (how's that for a segue?). The world knows this because I frequently talk about it as part of my own life journey. Sometimes charitably, sometimes less so. But as any Catholic knows, during Mass there is a homily. This is a fundamental part of any Mass. After the priest has read from one of the four Gospels in the New Testament (Matthew, Mark, Luke, or John), he then gives a homily, or what is called a sermon in other faiths. It's always based on the prescribed reading of the day and delivered from the ambo on the altar, known colloquially to some as a lectern (but there is a difference if you want to get technical, which I assume you don't). Some priests write their homily out and read it verbatim, while others have notes as reference points. Some use neither and speak extemporaneously. The prescribed instruction is for the priest to deliver his weekly homily from the ambo, but there are some priests who disregard that and come down closer to the congregation and deliver it there.

I appreciate the rules but absolutely love it when a priest breaks them (at least during the homily). The level of connection and relatability—areas where we'd all agree there's room for improvement with priests and their congregants—is vitally palpable through such proximate delivery when it happens. For those of you who are religious and attend any kind of services, you know exactly what I'm referring to.

Delivery from the heart, in any setting, is a winning formula. Except during a tax audit, but I digress.

Which is why I have used PowerPoint for the last time. In fact, of the 120 speeches I've delivered in the past two years, I've used a deck only three times, and that was because the client demanded it. Even then, I cut it down to three to four slides, *max*.

I've referenced the World Business Forum, produced by a group known as WOBI (World of Business Ideas) a couple of times in this book, as many of the Master Mentors featured in this book have presented there. I think it's the preeminent business conference in the United States, with a who's who of authors, business moguls, and retired but relevant political and military leaders on the roster. One year there was a speaker who is a household name as the CEO of a Fortune 50 tech company. She is someone whose career I have greatly admired, and I was especially excited to hear her speech. Now sometimes at WOBI, speakers will present behind a podium. Sometimes it's designed as a sit-down Q&A with the host, Chris Stanley. Other times the speaker will come to the middle of the stage or even down into the audience. I suspect it's all up to the comfort level and preference of the speaker.

This CEO took the stage with great anticipation.

But delivered a colossally disappointing performance.

This insanely accomplished, well-educated CEO proceeded during her precious forty-five minutes to march us through a trove of slides. I'd call it a death march if doing so wouldn't be a slam to death marches everywhere. The audience endured dozens of slides, and she could easily have done better without them. For those of you who've presented on large stages, you know we're often provided something known commonly as a "comfort monitor," "confidence monitor," or "downstage monitor." It's a video screen, about the size of a flat-screen television you might have in your bedroom, that typically illustrates three things: which slide you're currently showing to the audience, which slide is coming next, and the all-important countdown clock so you land on time (the only thing the event producer really cares about).

All I recall from her forty-five minutes was watching this renowned business leader looking down at her slides on the comfort monitor, slide advancer in hand, completely enslaved to the cadence of her slide deck. It's a harsh assessment, I know, but she lost all credibility with me—even though I knew she was brilliant. I silently pleaded with her to just trash the deck and tell us directly the amazing story of her company's success.

I could just imagine what went into her preparation. She was leading a massive multinational company with unrelatable demands and knew her WOBI speech was on the horizon. So a few weeks out, she gathered the corporate communications team and started building (drum roll, please) . . . a deck. Then, over the course of the coming days, she met with her team a few times and tightened it (which always means lengthening it). Maybe she walked through it in the company auditorium the day or night before. She likely even sat up in her hotel room that night (or morning of) and walked through each key point on every slide. Can you really communicate forty-seven key points in forty-five minutes?

Nope.

It was that day that I retired decks from my repertoire. Forever. Unless *forced* to do otherwise. And even then, you'll be able to count them on one hand.

Stop building decks. Inoculate yourself from the PowerPoint Plague and speak from the heart. Know your stuff so well that you don't need props. In the rare case a visual will transform your point for the audience, Nancy would argue to make it so spectacular that everyone remembers it forever. And if you must build a deck (really, a crutch), then build it as the last thing you do, not the first.

. . .

THE TRANSFORMATIONAL INSIGHT

PowerPoint is not the problem. Visuals aren't the problem. In fact, both are often quite useful to communicate a compelling vision. It's the sequence of building a deck as the component of designing your presentation that's the problem. First, structure the conversation by following the "what is and what could be . . . what is and what could be" framework. Then decide what visuals, if any, should be created to best drive home your point.

THE QUESTION

Are you willing to pay the price to know your subject so well, and bring it to life with your own storytelling skills, that you don't need a presentation crutch?

ERIC BARKER

FRANKLINCOVEY
ONLEADERSHIP
WITH SCOTT MILLER

EPISODE 15

ERIC BARKER
KNOWING YOUR STORY

The formula for bestselling books is complicated and always evolving. Beyond writing a valuable book that people want to read or listen to, you need a solid launch plan that includes strong social media engagement, book tours (live and virtual), publicity, appearing on every possible podcast (literally hundreds of them), and tireless radio and television interviews. You also need every friend from high school and college promoting it for you, all your colleagues and friends doing the same, and anything else you can think up. It also helps to have an impressive title and visually appealing book cover—"appealing" meaning the cover must look as good on a bookshelf as it does on a thumbnail-size image on a digital site, since between 80 and 90 percent of all books are now purchased through an online retailer. I love the local bookstore and I take my three boys weekly, but facts are facts when it comes to the future of book buying—it's nearly all digital.

One of the best book covers ever designed is Marie Forleo's *Everything Is Figureoutable.* Both her book and her *On Leadership* interview were so compelling, I will be featuring her in the second volume of *Master Mentors.*

I think one of the best book titles I've ever heard is Eric Barker's *Barking Up the Wrong Tree.* But beyond his catchy title, I thoroughly enjoyed his book and podcast interview. In fact, in nearly every podcast I join, I mention the power of his book. In *Barking Up the Wrong Tree: The Surprising Science Behind Why Everything You Know About Success Is (Mostly) Wrong,* Eric dispels many myths and bits of folklore about achieving success: nice guys finish last, the early bird gets the worm, and so on. His work is a truly fascinating look at how and why many of us believe certain ideas and what we thought were principles to live our lives by. Eric proves most of them are false and even blatant lies, and he encourages each of us to challenge the lies and myths we believe about ourselves—about our skills, our abilities, and our contributions.

What are the lies told about you that you believe and live yoked to? Or put another way, *What have I come to believe about me that someone well-intended, or perhaps less so, convinced me is true and doesn't need to be any longer?*

Bam!

That's an intriguing question, and one I think most people haven't taken the time to assess. In fact, the chapter could probably end here, but I feel compelled to add more. Just a tad, but it involves boxer shorts and a wire whisk.

Early in the launch of our weekly leadership podcast, we were, like any new podcast, searching for high-value guests. Our searching has lessened these days as we receive nonstop inquiries from agents, publicists, and potential guests themselves requesting an interview. One day in the beginning of the series, I was preparing for an interview with the famed celebrity actress and producer Viola Davis. Yes, *that* Viola Davis—recipient of an Academy

Award, an Emmy Award, and two Tony Awards. In my research for the interview, I came across a passage in one of Brené Brown's books where Viola talked about her early upbringing. She was raised in what many would term extreme poverty. In her younger years, she never knew when she came home from school if the lights would be on or the water would be running. Some days it wasn't. Viola would head to school unbathed, and you can imagine how the other students reacted and treated her. It was humiliating. Humbling. Perhaps emboldening, even.

Later in life, Viola became an actress and moved to Hollywood. Her friends told her she'd better get a thick skin. That's something I can relate to in my life—I've intentionally developed "thick skin" as a coping method for criticism. I bet many of you can probably relate as well.

Viola says about this, "They tell you to develop a thick skin so things don't get to you. What they don't tell you is that your thick skin will keep everything from getting out, too. Love, intimacy, vulnerability. I don't want that. Thick skin doesn't work anymore. I want to be transparent and translucent."[1]

Profound.

Then she continued and talked about the power of "owning your story." What the hell does that mean? Owning your story? That sounded rather foreign to me, like Reiki, yoga, sound bowls, and other non–Scott Miller stuff.

I didn't give it another thought.

Until the next day.

I was taping the podcast interview with Eric Barker. At the end of our conversation, he referenced the value of "owning your story."

Are you kidding me? Twice in two days?

So, that night after my taping with Eric, I'm in bed with my wife. All three sons are upstairs asleep and I lean over to her and ask, "Stephanie, have you ever told yourself your story?"

Now it's ten-ish, and she leans over and musters a profound, "Huh?"

I repeat, "Have you ever told yourself your story? You know, like your life's journey? What you've done? What you still want to do? What you believe and what you question about yourself? The mistakes you've made and what you're proud and even ashamed of?"

I'm now energized around this topic and she's . . . asleep.

Hmmm . . .

I lie there for a minute before getting out of bed and walk toward the kitchen. It's now almost ten thirty, and I'm wearing (sorry for the visual) a pair of plaid, flannel Ralph Lauren boxer shorts, and nothing else as I head to the kitchen and grab a giant wire whisk.

Why a wire whisk? I'm going to use it as a microphone, of course. To interview myself.

So, at forty-nine, I tell myself my story for the first time in my life. Alone, out loud and uncensored, in the dark, with nobody listening, I conducted the interview as I walked in circles around my living room for over an hour. This was nearly four years ago, but it's viscerally burned in my mind and always will be.

It began something like this: My name is Scott Jeffrey Miller. I am forty-nine years old. I live in Salt Lake City. I am married with three sons—four, six, and eight. I am the chief marketing officer for FranklinCovey and have worked there for twenty-two years. I was born in Winter Park, Florida, in a solidly middle-class family. I have a brother four years older than me and who is the favorite son. My father's father died of cancer when my dad was only ten years old. My father's twin brother contracted polio while in high school and spent years suffering in an iron lung until he finally succumbed. As a result, my grandmother was in mourning for the rest of her life—fifty years.

My father really didn't have parents.

My mother was an only child, and both of her parents were alcoholics. They moved often, mainly because of the uncertainty created from their addictions, and were, as it's been told, always one step ahead of their furniture and appliances being repossessed. I hear one of them may have accidentally taken their own life, but it's not talked about in our home, so I may be wrong.

My mother really didn't have parents.

In the sixth grade, my elementary school principal, Mr. Wiley, decided he was going to separate the grades into three levels: advanced, average, and slow. Seriously? Are you a sociopath, Mr. Wiley? Slow . . . ? Skinny Scott Miller drew the short straw and entered a multiyear academic life of Slow. Pardon my language readers, "ARE YOU F'ING KIDDING ME? SLOW?" What does an eleven-year-old do with that?

I am a lifelong stutterer. I stutter. Since early in life, I've had a speech therapist and endured countless speech-pathologist sessions. Braces. Twice. Head gear. NERD ALERT! I still wear a retainer nightly to keep my teeth from interrupting my already difficult speech patterns. I slur my words constantly, and to this day, employ two separate speech coaches to keep myself decipherable onstage.

I took Algebra 1 three times in high school and never even made it to geometry. In college, I took statistics three times and finally passed when a professor, who took a liking to me, saw that I had other talents waiting to bloom. He let me write a paper on Chinese/Taiwanese relations, and if I used an abundance of statistics in it, he agreed to pass me. D+ as I recall.

And then that night, I confessed to myself, out loud (because you know I'm Catholic), all the other sins, shortcomings, and mistakes I'd made in life. I followed it with all the negative things I thought about myself and then pondered why I thought them. I unpacked more, still walking in circles, holding the microphone-whisk and telling myself what I believed about me. I then further unpacked *why* I believed them, who told me what, and what their motivation must have been.

And then, when I decided I was done, I sort of just flipped into—and this is a phrase I have never typed or spoken—*self-love*. I decided to start liking myself—loving myself. Finally, at the age of forty-nine.

I then told myself all the great things I believed about me and finally discounted all the lies I'd come to believe. I acknowledged some weren't actually lies, but I was going to move into the next day proving them wrong and out of date.

The next day, I landed a weekly radio program on iHeart radio. A slow stutterer with a radio program. Imagine that, Mr. Wiley. Then I was awarded a book deal and wrote, over the next seven months, *Management Mess to Leadership Success*. It spent six consecutive weeks at #1 on Amazon and won BookPal's Outstanding Works of Literature Award in the leadership category. I launched a podcast next and realized other feats of greatness (abounding humility is not one of them) that don't need to be listed here.

You get the point. Telling myself my story actually started the next chapter in that story. And not just any chapter, but a series of chapters that has set up the second half of my life to be, perhaps, my greatest. You see, you don't tell yourself your story to memorialize the past—you tell yourself your story to pivot toward a new and enticing future.

So thank you, Viola Davis. And thank you, Eric Barker.

. . .

THE TRANSFORMATIONAL INSIGHT

Stop your story. Stop the tape. Whose story are you living? Yours, or Mr. Wiley's?

THE QUESTION

Are you willing, tonight, to put down *Master Mentors* and go into your kitchen (I don't care what you're wearing) and grab a whisk, or a wooden spoon, or a spatula? Doesn't matter. Tell yourself your story. Alone. In the dark. With nobody listening. Out loud. Uncensored. You may be on the cusp of starting the next chapter in your own story.

CONCLUSION

This book began with the transformational insight of gratitude and ended with the power of knowing your story. Those are fitting bookends from our journey through the wisdom of thirty Master Mentors, and I suggest it's worth reflecting on each of them one last time—the principles, practices, traits, and strategies that made every transformational insight an important part of this collection:

Nick Vujicic—Gratitude
Stephanie McMahon—Your Brand Is How You Show Up
Dave Hollis—Vulnerability
Susan David—Emotional Agility
Daniel Pink—Peak, Trough, and Recovery
Karen Dillon—Deliberate vs. Emergent Strategies
Anne Chow—What's Your Motive?
Chris McChesney—Keep a Compelling Scoreboard
Daniel Amen—Protect Your Brain
General Stanley McChrystal—Be on the Right Side of History
Kim Scott—Radical Candor
Dorie Clark—Twist If You Can't Invent (And Even If You Can)
Bob Whitman—The Servant Leader
Susan Cain—Rethinking Introverts and Extroverts
Ryan Holiday—Self-Discipline

Nely Galán—Hype Your Failures
Leif Babin—Extreme Ownership
Stedman Graham—Choose Your Identity
Liz Wiseman—Be a Multiplier and Not a Diminisher
Jay Papasan—The ONE Thing
Seth Godin—Fearless vs. Reckless
Todd Davis—The Power of Relationships
Donald Miller—Clarify Your Message
M.J. Fièvre—Balancing Efficiency with Effectiveness
Whitney Johnson—Disrupt Yourself
Trent Shelton—The Power Perspective
Brendon Burchard—Prolific Quality Output
Stephen M. R. Covey—Pulling the Plug
Nancy Duarte—The PowerPoint Plague
Eric Barker—Knowing Your Story

As you've no doubt experienced, each transformational insight is worthy of its own deeper dive and further engagement with the Master Mentor behind it. You could easily choose one at random, work to incorporate the insight into your personal and professional life, and you would find that it yielded demonstrably positive results. But if I may suggest, pick several from the list above without overthinking it. Consider which transformational insight tugs at you as the potential solution to a stifling weakness; which ignites your creativity and drive to do something different; and which, if adopted, could elevate a dormant strength into a powerful force working on your behalf.

I'm certain that as you use this book, not as an end but as a beginning, you will experience the similarly profound insights that have had a powerful effect in my life. I may not have truly mastered any of them, but they rise as a North Star toward which—*to* which—I can diligently navigate. So, as the bookend topics suggest, begin with an abundant sense of gratitude for all the "get tos" in your life. Then be intentional about the story that is you and what the turning of the next chapter will entail. What transformational insights will provide fodder for the ongoing journey that is now up to you. May they help take you exactly where you want and deserve to go. And, just as important, I thank the thirty friends featured here for their abundance, vulnerability, and willingness to not just appear on our podcast, but to allow me the creative license to select an insight that not just resonated with me, but that I thought would with others as well.

Looking forward to *Master Mentors Volume II* . . . see you there!

ENDNOTES

Daniel Pink · Peak, Trough, and Recovery

1. Samuel E. Jones, et al, "Genome-Wide Association Analyses of Chronotype in 697,828 Individuals Provides Insights into Circadian Rhythms," *Nature Communications* 10, no. 1 (January 2019), p. 343. Accessed at doi:10.1038/s41467-018-08259-7.

Karen Dillon · Deliberate vs. Emergent Strategies

1. Dan Rockwell. "93% of Successful Companies Abandon Their Original Strategy," Leadership Freak, January 10, 2017. Accessed at https://leadershipfreak.blog/2017/01/10/93-of-successful-companies-abandon-their-original-strategy/.

Chris McChesney · Keep a Compelling Scoreboard

1. Jim Harter, "Employee Engagement on the Rise in the U.S.," Gallup.com, August 26, 2018. Accessed at https://news.gallup.com/poll/241649/employee-engagement-rise.aspx.
2. Alyssa Retallick, "The Cost of a Disengaged Employee," US | Glassdoor for Employers, May 25, 2015. Accessed at https://www.glassdoor.com/employers/blog/the-cost-of-a-disengaged-employee/.

General Stanley McChrystal · Be on the Right Side of History

1. Dexter Filkins, "McChrystal Is Summoned to Washington over Remarks," CNBC, June 22, 2010, https://www.cnbc.com/2010/06/22/mcchrystal-is-summoned-to-washington-over-remarks.html.

2. Elizabeth A. Harris, "Simon & Schuster Names Dana Canedy New Publisher," *New York Times*, July 6, 2020. Accessed at https://www.nytimes.com/2020/07/06/books/dana-canedy-named-simon-schuster-publisher.html.

Dorie Clark · Twist if You Can't Invent (And Even If You Can)

1. Malcolm Gladwell, *The Tipping Point: How Little Things Can Make a Big Difference*, Kindle edition (New York: Little, Brown & Company, 2013), p. 38.

Susan Cain · Rethinking Introverts and Extroverts

1. Julie Rains, "Insights from *Quiet: The Power of Introverts*," Working to Live Differently, November 26, 2018. Accessed at https://www.workingtolive.com/insights-from-quiet-the-power-of-introverts/.

Nely Galán · Hype Your Failures

1. *On Leadership with Scott Miller*, "Episode #29 Nely Galán." SoundCloud, FranklinCovey, 2020. Accessed at https://soundcloud.com/onleadership/episode-29-nely-galan.

Leif Babin · Extreme Ownership

1. *On Leadership with Scott Miller*, "Episode #75 Leif Babin." SoundCloud, FranklinCovey, 2020. Accessed at https://soundcloud.com/onleadership/episode-75-leif-babin.
2. *On Leadership with Scott Miller*, "Episode #75 Leif Babin."

Stedman Graham · Choose Your Identity

1. Stedman Graham, *Identity: Your Passport to Success* (Financial Times/Prentice Hall, 2012), p. 3.
2. Stedman Graham, *Identity*, p. 3.
3. Stedman Graham, *Identity Leadership: To Lead Others You Must First Lead Yourself* (Center Street, 2019).

Jay Papasan · The ONE Thing

1. Gary Keller and Jay Papasan, *The One Thing: The Surprisingly Simple Truth Behind Extraordinary Results*, Kindle edition (Austin, TX: Bard Press, 2017), p. 9.
2. Gary Keller and Jay Papasan, *The One Thing*, p. 25.

Brendon Burchard · Prolific Quality Output

1. Brendon Burchard, "High Performance Habits: Excerpts," Brendon.com, April 3, 2020. Accessed at https://brendon.com/blog/high-performance habits/.
2. Brendon Burchard, *High Performance Habits: How Extraordinary People Become That Way* (Carlsbad, CA: Hay House, Inc., 2017).

Eric Barker · Knowing Your Story

1. Brené Brown, "Courage and Power from Pain: An Interview with Viola Davis," Brenebrown.com, June 27, 2019. Accessed at https://brenebrown .com/blog/2018/05/09/courage-power-pain-interview-viola-davis/.

INDEX

ABOUT THE AUTHOR

Capping a twenty-five-year career in which he served as chief marketing officer and executive vice president, Scott Miller currently serves as FranklinCovey's senior advisor on thought leadership, leading the strategy, development, and publication of the firm's bestselling books on thought leadership.

Miller hosts the FranklinCovey-sponsored *On Leadership with Scott Miller*, the world's largest and fastest-growing weekly leadership podcast, reaching more than six million people. Miller also authors a leadership column for Inc.com and *Utah Business*, and hosted the weekly iHeart Radio show *Great Life, Great Career.*

Miller is the author of the multivolume *Mess to Success* series, including *Management Mess to Leadership Success: 30 Challenges to Become the Leader You Would Follow*, *Marketing Mess to Brand Success,* and the forthcoming *Job Mess to Career Success* (January 2022). He is the coauthor of the *Wall Street Journal* bestseller *Everyone Deserves a Great Manager: The 6 Critical Practices for Leading a Team* and the author of *Master Mentors: 30 Transformative Insights from Our Greatest Minds*, which features insights from his interviews with the leading thinkers of our time, including Seth Godin, Susan Cain, General Stanley McChrystal, and many others.

In addition to supporting FranklinCovey's global thought leadership efforts, Miller has developed the **ignite your genius™** coaching series to help leaders take their careers from accidental to deliberate. He hosts FranklinCovey's Bookclub.com series with world-renowned authors.

Prior to his roles as chief marketing officer and executive vice president of business development, Scott served as general manager and client partner in FranklinCovey's Chicago and UK offices. As a highly sought-after speaker and podcast guest, he has presented to hundreds of audiences across every industry and loves to share his unique journey as an unfiltered leader thriving in today's highly filtered corporate culture.

Miller began his professional career in 1992 with the Disney Development Company (the real estate development division of Walt Disney Company) as a founding member of the development team that designed the town of Celebration, Florida.

Miller and his wife live in Salt Lake City, Utah, with their three sons.

About FranklinCovey

Franklin Covey Co. (NYSE: FC) is a global, public company, specializing in organizational performance improvement. We help organizations achieve results that require lasting changes in human behavior. Our world-class solutions enable greatness in individuals, teams and organizations and are accessible through the FranklinCovey All Access Pass®. They are available across multiple modalities and in 20 plus languages. Clients have included the Fortune 100, Fortune 500, thousands of small- and mid-sized businesses, numerous government entities, and educational institutions. FranklinCovey has more than 100 direct and partner offices providing professional services in more than 160 countries and territories.